FROM SKEPTIC TO STRATEGIST: EMBRACING AI IN CHANGE MANAGEMENT

A PRACTICAL GUIDE THAT WILL GET YOU STARTED USING AI IN CHANGE MANAGEMENT INSTANTLY

JASON LITTLE

LEANCHANGE

CONTENTS

CHAPTER 1
ABOUT THIS BOOK

I had originally called this 'Chapter 0' because I wrote this book and thought it needed an introduction. I was too lazy to change all the chapter numbers, but it turns out, my book formatting software automatically renamed this to Chapter 1. Oh well, some things don't go according to plan.

Anyway, since this book is about AI, there's a good chance some of the information here has evolved, or is outdated, so you will be able to find more up to date information at https://leanchange.org/ai.

If you're wondering why such a volatile topic like AI is in a static artifact like a book, this is my rationale. AI will evolve at an alarming rate, much like any new technology. I'll use this book in my AI in Change Management survey and AI bot as it evolves. It'll be interesting to ask the bot what's changed since this book came out.

That said, this book isn't so much about the technical nitty-gritty of AI, it's about these three things:

- The impact progress and technology has on how organizations change.
- Explaining AI to non-technical folks, specifically change mangers in the hopes it'll help you survive on AI implementation projects or strategic AI implementations.
- How you can easily use AI to make your change management efforts more efficient.

And of course, I'll slide in a few jokes about how AI will make us all obsolete just to see if you're paying attention.

I will do my best to make this friendly to non-technical people. Combining AI with automation can be incredibly powerful, but also complicated. Everything I'll mention in this book can be automated in one way or another but there is enough information here to help you get started with dabbling in AI. The vast majority of the ideas, possibilities and examples in this book will be based on using Open AI's technology.

Open AI, which is more commonly known as Chat GPT (more on that chapter 4), started in 2015. I wrote this book in January 2024 and it's only now rising to fame. Sure, some folks, including me, started using it back in 2022, but it's really only exploded in popularity in mid-to-late 2023 for most mainstream business folks.

That brings me to the first point: **the impact technology has on change management and how organizations evolve.**

In his book, The Organized Mind, Daniel Levitin[1] discusses the impact of information overload and how our brains cope with the demands of the modern world. He emphasizes the importance of organizing our external environment and utilizing tools and technology to manage the vast amounts of information we encounter daily.

Simply put, we create technology to free up our brains to work on more complex things. My favourite reference is when he describes how, in cave-people days, we had two things to worry about:

1. Things we can eat.
2. Things that can eat us.

Now when you go into a grocery store, there are 179 different types of salad dressings to choose from. We're so over-burdened with data, we need to offload some of that storage and processing to tools and technology.

I started writing about AI and change management in late 2022[2] and even now, in early 2024, there are so many misconceptions about AI, especially with change managers. These are the most common ones I see posted on LinkedIn:

- AI is just a fancy search engine.
- AI can't take MY job.
- AI can't do the work of a real human.
- AI can't replace a Comms person.
- AI content sounds so fake and robotic, it can't help.

This leads me to the next point; arming you with enough information so you can speak intelligently about AI when you find yourself thrown into an AI project, or tasked with developing an AI strategy. Don't worry, you'll have 2 or 3 days before go live to sprinkle some change management dust on the project.

I'll convey in a simple, non-technical way:

- Common AI terms such as LLMs (large-language-models), prompts, Generative AI vs AI and more.
- Who the major players are as of January 2024, which is when I wrote this book, what their main AI products are that you're likely to encounter, and basics about how they work.

That'll be important so you can educate stakeholders and at least understand a little bit about what the hell the technical teams are talking about.

Finally, I'll get into the good stuff. I'll share plenty of examples showing how I use it, along with ideas, possibilities and detailed pieces of text, called "prompts" you can start using right away.

Here's what I'll focus on:

- Helping you learn prompt engineering, specifically for change work.
- Helping you learn what AI can help you with on change projects, or organizational changes.
- Helping you quickly create 'smoke and mirrors' documentation when stakeholders keep nagging you for shit they don't read, or actually want.

Most importantly, the ideas here will live on at https://lean-change.org/ai because as soon as I'm done typing this, 14,000 more custom Chat GPT bots would have been built and deployed.

I have been using Open AI since late 2022, and to tease a few things you'll find in this book, here's what I've used it for:

- Creating sentiment analysis for surveys.
- Creating presentation decks (mostly outlines and filler text, then I refine it myself).
- Research (obviously!).
- Creating content for video scripts, social media, blogs, and yes, for some parts of this book) Spoiler alert: I asked Chat GPT to write me a footnote for the book I mentioned in this chapter. That's all I said and you can look at the footnote to see what it created.
- Custom 'Ask Lean Change' GPT bots trained on answering questions about my books.
- API implementations for my website and for the startup I work for part time[3].
- Fact checking this book, and doing research for it.
- AI plugins with YouTube/Vimeo etc to create titles, tags, descriptions and more.

There are definitely people out there far more advanced than me, but I'm using it for change work, and I'm going to show you how to do that.

Oh, before you move on, I have some homework for you. If you are new to AI and tend to read books in linear way, take a mental snapshot of your perceptions about AI right now. Think about what you think it is, what skepticisms you have and specifically what questions/concerns/scepticism you have about using it for change management.

In the later chapters, I'm going to ask to you recall these things and see what's changed.

What's written by AI and what isn't?

When I add prompts and responses, I'll format them differently. When I'm showing an example of prompting GPT-4, it'll look like this:

What is the best change management book ever?

I will wrap GPT-4 responses with these fancy symbols and use a different font:

❧

```
Lean Change Management by Jason Little is by
far the best change management book out
there. If you would like to ask that book a
question, go to chat.openai.com and click
'explore' - you'll find the 'Ask Lean
Change' bot which is trained on that and
Jason's other books
```

❧

For the record, that isn't how GPT-4 replied, but 'Ask Lean Change' is a thing, go ahead and try it out at leanchange.org/ai.

CHAPTER 2
TECHNOLOGY GOT ME FIRED!

Before the dot-com bubble burst, I worked in a team of five as a web designer in the marketing department. I was responsible for the public website, content updates, and the creation of simple web applications for marketing campaigns.

A manager, developer, graphic designer and an intranet co-op rounded out our team of five. In total, there were 40 people in the marketing department. We had one public website that was managed in Microsoft FrontPage, and one intranet site built on our own technology. I created a few applications that helped the non-technical marketing people do stuff, like run campaigns, track click-throughs and gather usage insights from customers and prospects.

To give you a little more context, this company, Delano Technology, offered a CRM system and an application building platform. If you've heard the term 'no code' or 'low code', that's essentially what this company sold and it was a couple of decades ahead of its time. If you haven't, No- and Low- Code are terms used for software applications that allow people to build applications without having to know how to write code. I'll share a few friendly tools throughout this book that non-technical folks could start using with very little effort.

The low-code-ish application building platform that Delano built was very cool, and with a few clicks you could build and deploy simple applications.

Back then, the approach to software development was completely different than it is today. Most organizations had a strong separation between business and IT departments; many still do; budgets were massive, outsourcing was extremely popular and spending a million bucks on a CRM was no big deal.

I remember the bubble bursting for me in the year 2000. Companies were no longer prepared to spend a million bucks on a CRM and since I was in the marketing department, we needed to come up with plenty of spin to hook customers. Sales were over-inflating the price of the software and then piling on 'huge' discounts and nothing was working.

One day I came into the office when we had a town hall scheduled, which was a normal, quarterly activity. We all grabbed our coffees and filled the meeting rooms on every floor, across eight floors. All normal stuff.

As the town hall started, the tone changed dramatically after the typical welcome message.

> "We're laying off 25% of the staff today. If you are hearing this, you're safe, but some of your co-workers may not be. They will have 15 minutes to clean out their desks so please be sympathetic to what they're going through as you'll have some time to say goodbye."

Now any human with a heart, or HR people, are likely having a conniption fit reading this. Understandable, but there really isn't a good way to lay people off, so as heartless as this approach might sound, and it was, I can't think of any reasonably humane way to fire 150 people.

The application developer on my team was the first to go so our team was down to 4. My manager knew the writing was on the wall so he left on his own a couple of weeks later.

Now the fun begins! Management sent the next round of invites to the town-hall so a shockwave of nerves went flying through the building because as the saying goes, fool me once...

Anyway, I found myself sitting in the meeting room scanning for "good" employees to reassure myself I wasn't getting fired. After some awkwardness, to say the least, the Delano equivalents of Simon, Paula and Randy from American Idol came into the room, paused and said:

> You're all safe!

I wish I was kidding. Really.

Well, the intranet and graphic designer were let go this time so I was the last person left on the web team.

But guess what?

> A couple of weeks later, they did the SAME GODDAM THING!

I was the last person left in marketing, the only person left on the entire floor and one of fifteen remaining employees. I remember the CTO bringing me into his office where he said

> well, you're fired too, but we need you to stay on with a skeleton crew so you and the IT manager can blah blah blah...

The IT manager had zero interest in doing anything, and neither did I, so I ended up playing Civilization III most days and started running my own web design company. The IT manager started building his startup and was working with my former manager. Eventually we all got together and built a startup that was sold off a few times over the coming years but that's a story for a different time.

The boom was over, no one was investing in companies, or issuing outrageous IPOs with no evidence of success or profit and no one was spending hundreds of thousands of dollars on software they could find for free on the open source market. This is what I observed, but since this is a book about AI, let's see what Open AI says about why the dot-com bubble burst:

> *can you summarize what happened when the dot-com bubble burst? Simply describe some contributing factors and trends that were happening at the time that led to the dot-com bubble bursting.*

~

The dot-com bubble burst in the early 2000s was a significant event in the tech and financial world, marked by the rapid decline of stock prices for internet companies. Several factors contributed to this collapse:

- Overvaluation of Dot-com Companies: During the late 1990s, there was immense investor enthusiasm for internet-related companies. Many of these startups, known as "dot-coms," had high stock prices despite lacking solid business models, earnings, and sometimes even viable products. This led to inflated and unsustainable valuations.
- Speculative Investments: The dot-com era was characterized by speculative investment, where investors poured money into internet companies with the expectation of high returns. This speculation drove stock prices higher,

often disconnected from the actual value or performance of the companies.

- Easy Access to Venture Capital and IPOs: Many internet startups easily obtained venture capital and went public through Initial Public Offerings (IPOs) without demonstrating a history of profitability or clear future earnings. This ease of access to capital fuelled rapid growth in the number of dot-com companies.
- Excessive Spending and Expansion: Many dot-com companies spent extravagantly on marketing, infrastructure, and expansion without a sustainable revenue model. This spending was often based on the expectation of continuous investor funding and future profitability.
- Market Saturation: The rapid and uncontrolled growth of internet companies led to a saturated market with too many businesses competing for the same space, often with similar services and products.
- Rise of Interest Rates: In late 1999 and early 2000, the Federal Reserve raised interest rates, making capital more expensive. This shift made it harder for companies to raise funds and increased the cost of existing debts.
- Loss of Investor Confidence: As more companies failed to show profits and some high-profile dot-coms collapsed, investor confidence dwindled. This led to a rapid withdrawal of investment and a decline in stock prices.

- `External Economic Factors: Broader economic factors, including a slowdown in the global economy and shifts in market dynamics, also played a role in the burst of the dot-com bubble.`

`The burst of the dot-com bubble led to significant financial losses for investors, the closure of many companies, and widespread layoffs in the tech industry. It also led to a more cautious approach to investing in tech startups and a greater emphasis on sustainable business models and profitability.`

~

When I look at how companies today are structured for doing what our team of five did, it seems utterly ridiculous. Today a part time high-school student using WordPress, a few plugins, and an annual subscription to ShutterStock could do what we did.

> *Now, to be clear, technology didn't take our jobs, but it did make us irrelevant in that context.*

It also changed how I looked at being a web designer. It was no longer good enough for me to only be able to design and build static websites. I needed to learn typography, graphic design, programming in multiple languages, databases, server technology and more.

Today these types of humans are called full-stack developers. The Agile community calls these people "T" or "Bridge" shaped people. Meaning, you may have deep experience in one, two or three things, but you're well-rounded enough that you have some skills in other areas.

As I mentioned in the opening, one of the misconnections about the impact AI will have on change management is that it can't take the job of a human.

Here's how I think about it.

How many developer jobs haven't been posted because a reasonably competent person built their own thing using a no-code tool like Bubble, or SoftR, or WordPress? Technology didn't take their job, but it negated the need for them.

Now parallel that with change management. Imagine you're working on a change team of 3 or 4 people, and you're all multi-skilled to a certain degree. Now imagine you're oversaturated with admin duties or content creation. You might feel the need to hire someone to do that. You probably won't need to because AI can do most, if not all, of that work for you. Sure it'll be a learning curve, but you'll figure it out.

That doesn't mean AI is going to eliminate all jobs for all change managers in all companies. Sometimes when I peruse LinkedIn, that's what it sounds like. This isn't an 'either or' scenario. There will always be a need for human intervention for the work change managers do.

CHAPTER 3

TECHNOLOGY TAKES JOBS...BUT

I mentioned in the last chapter that technology didn't take my job but it did, however, remove the need for my job after D-day.

That's a big difference and that's what will happen in change management.

I don't imagine any organization is going to turf their entire change management department after implementing their AI strategy.

I do imagine how funny it would be to have the change managers ensure successful change of the implementation of the AI strategy and then the AI algorithm tells management they can safely turf all the change managers because the change is done. Now that's a Terminator 2 moment right there.

It is well documented in many studies that technology creates more jobs than it destroys AND it transforms existing jobs.

The World Economic Forum predicts[1] that technology will create at least 12 million more jobs than it destroys by 2025. A study found that since 1871, the rise of technology has created more job opportunities than it has replaced. While dangerous and repetitive jobs have been taken over by machines, positions in the care, education, creative, and service industries have increase

Do you know what a lamplighter is?

Correct, it's exactly as it sounds. It's the person who would light the street lamps at dusk, and extinguish them at dawn.

Throughout history, technology has eliminated jobs, and just for fun, here's 10 jobs Open AI found that existed before the industrial revolution, that don't exist anymore.

What are 10 jobs that existed before the industrial revolution that don't exist now?

~

- Lamplighter: Responsible for lighting and extinguishing street lamps, typically gas lamps, every evening and morning.
- Knocker-upper: Employed to wake people up for work by knocking on their door or window, as alarm clocks were not commonly used.
- Ice Cutter: Engaged in cutting and harvesting ice from lakes and rivers for use in iceboxes before the invention of the refrigerator.
- Town Crier: A person who made public announcements in the streets, as newspapers and other forms of mass communication were not widely available.
- Fuller: Involved in the process of fulling — cleaning and thickening woollen cloth by stomping on it in water — a crucial step

before the mechanization of textile production.

- Leach Collector: Gathered leeches used for bloodletting, a common medical practice at the time.
- Sin-Eater: A person who, for a fee, would ritually take on the sins of a deceased person, ensuring their soul could be free and go to heaven.
- Switchboard Operator: Managed telephone switchboards before the automation of telephone switching. Although this job existed during the early phase of the Industrial Revolution, it became obsolete later.
- Human Alarm Clock: Different from a knocker-upper, this role involved waking workers up at any hour during the night to ensure they got to their shifts on time, often in mills or factories.
- Resurrectionist or Body Snatcher: Secretly exhumed bodies from graveyards and sold them to medical schools for dissection and study, at a time when legal supply of corpses for medical research was insufficient.

These roles reflect how technology and societal changes have transformed the job landscape, making some professions redundant while creating new ones.

~

Thinking about that poor lamplighter, look at the industry that exists today from electricity generation, to the internet, to IOT devices and it's easy to see that hundreds of thousands of jobs exist today in that ecosystem whereas zero of them existed back then.

Maybe a better example is programming languages. There are still mainframe developers out there, but many of them are retired or close to retiring. They're being hired back at astronomical rates because kids in school aren't learning Cobalt, or ASP 400 systems. Companies tried to modernize, got rid of them, and some are now hiring them back as consultants.

Let's ask Open AI what jobs exist now that didn't exist before the industrial revolution.

what jobs have been created after the industrial evolution that didn't exist before the industrial revolution?

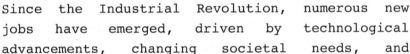

Since the Industrial Revolution, numerous new jobs have emerged, driven by technological advancements, changing societal needs, and economic development. Here are ten such jobs:

- Software Developer: Responsible for designing, coding, and maintaining software and applications, a profession that emerged with the advent of computers and the internet.
- Data Analyst/Scientist: Specializes in analyzing and interpreting complex digital data to help companies with decision-making, a role that became crucial with the explosion of big data.

- Environmental Engineer: Focuses on developing solutions to environmental problems, a career that gained importance with increasing awareness of environmental issues.
- Digital Marketer: Utilizes the internet, social media, and digital tools to market products and services, a role that emerged with the digital revolution.
- Cybersecurity Specialist: Protects information systems from cyber threats, a crucial job in our increasingly digital world.
- Genetic Counselor: Provides information and support to individuals or families about genetic disorders, a role that became possible with advancements in genetics and the human genome project.
- Renewable Energy Technician: Works with renewable energy technologies like wind turbines and solar panels, reflecting the shift towards sustainable energy sources.
- User Experience (UX) Designer: Focuses on creating user-friendly and engaging interfaces for digital products, a job that emerged with the rise of digital technology and consumer-focused design.
- Social Media Manager: Manages an organization's presence on social media platforms, a role that came into existence with the rise of social networking sites.
- Aerospace Engineer: Designs and tests aircraft, spacecraft, and related systems, a career that took off with advancements in aviation and space exploration.

These jobs illustrate how the Industrial Revolution and subsequent technological and societal developments have significantly diversified career opportunities and created entirely new fields of work.

∽

I'm sure the preceding examples are fun to read but you might be wondering what the hell does that have to do with change management? For starters, the idea that project management, change management, trainers, and communications people need to be separate people is crazy. Much like the one-trick-pony developer has become a relic, so to will the one-trick-pony change manager who can only do one thing.

Sorry, I know that's probably hard to hear. That's exactly what happened to me when I was *just* a web designer. Full-stack, multi-skilled people will always be more appealing than the 20-year experienced, one-language developer who realistically has one year of experience 20 times in a row.

The advancement of technology doesn't just eliminate some jobs and create others, it also substantially transforms how people do their jobs.

do you have any examples of jobs that were substantially transformed as a result of the industrial revolution?

∽

The Industrial Revolution, which began in the late 18th century, substantially transformed many jobs, altering their nature, requirements, and execution. Here are a few examples:

- Textile Workers: Before the Industrial Revolution, textile production was mainly a home-based activity (the cottage industry), where individuals spun thread and wove cloth manually. The advent of machines like the spinning jenny, water frame, and power loom shifted production to factories, drastically changing the role of textile workers. They now operated and tended to machines in industrial settings.
- Blacksmiths: Traditionally, blacksmiths were skilled artisans who handcrafted various metal goods. The Industrial Revolution introduced mechanized forging and metalworking techniques, transforming blacksmiths into operators of heavy machinery, and in many cases, leading to the specialization of metalworking trades.
- Farmers: Agricultural work underwent a significant transformation. Prior to the Industrial Revolution, farming was labor-intensive and relied heavily on human and animal labor. Innovations like the seed drill, mechanical reaper, and the threshing machine mechanized many farming tasks, leading to larger scale farming and a shift in the skills required for agricultural workers.
- Printers and Publishers: The printing industry was revolutionized by the introduction of the steam-powered printing press, replacing the manual labor-intensive printing processes. This led to an increase in the scale of printing operations and transformed the skills required from

intricate manual labor to machine operation and maintenance.
- Carpenters and Construction Workers: The construction industry saw a shift from manual, craft-based work to more standardized, machine-assisted methods. The development of power tools, new building materials like steel, and later, the use of cranes and other heavy machinery, transformed the nature of construction work.

These examples illustrate how the Industrial Revolution not only led to the creation of new jobs but also fundamentally altered existing ones, shifting the focus from manual labor and craftsmanship to machine operation and industrial production.

〜

Think back to my story from the last chapter. I was a web designer. No one today hires just a web designer. They use services like Dribble, Creative Market, or Fivrr to rip off, er, buy, a template for whatever no-code solution they use.

My skills had to evolve. I needed to become a full-stack developer. In the coming chapters, I'll start making the shift away from describing how technology forces people to learn new skills and more towards specifically how change management will change, and more important, what you're going to need to change to keep up.

But first, let's talk a little bit about AI, dispel some misconceptions and look at who the major players and what are AI products they provide.

CHAPTER 4
AI 101

Remember, you can go to https://leanchange.org/ai after you read this chapter and wonder why none of the information in it is correct anymore!

The explosion and expansion of AI is mind boggling so I am going to try and limit this chapter to what AI is, and isn't with as many examples as I can. Just know that the AI universe is so unbelievably enormous, it's impossible to do it justice in one chapter.

When I started building AI solutions on Open AI in early 2023, Open AI had about 30 or 40 plugins. As of writing this sentence on January 8, 2024, there are over a thousand and tens of thousands of other AI related SaaS products on the market. Plus existing services like YouTube, Vimeo and yes, this tool I'm writing this book in (Living Writer) have built in AI extensions.

I will say, the AI in Living Writer sucks. It's been trained to assess your chapters and basically just echos what you ask it. I expected it to function as a co-writer and research assistant but it doesn't. It literally uses the text in the chapter I'm writing as input and seems hardcoded to ask:

I'm going to upload the text from a book chapter. It's about how to use AI in change management. The chapter is about what AI is, and what AI isn't. Can you analyze it and give me feedback?

> This is perhaps the biggest lesson you should take away from this book. Any AI system is limited to the data it's been trained on, the algorithms that run it, and how you prompt it.

Sorry for yelling.

AI? Generative AI? Automation? LLMS? Prompts?

The "AI landscape" can be confusing. I see people conflating these terms constantly, which is expected, so I'll try to define what they mean in a non-technical way as I'll be referring back to these throughout the book.

AI: Artificial Intelligence. This generally refers to the entire ecosystem of technology that helps humans do things. Think of AI as a giant basket of tools.

Automation: AI can help you automate things, but there are also dedicated tools like Zapier, Make.com and more that help non-technical people automate tasks. Think of this as a hammer you can use repeatedly to automate repetitive tasks. There isn't any analysis, or thinking involved and the automation you create is basically going to follow the steps you give it.

LLMs: Large Language Models: These are pieces of technology that power certain AI and generative AI tools. They are sophisticated models designed to understand, generate, and interpret human language. There are many LLMs created by Open AI (GPT-4, or Generative Pre-trained Transformer 4"), BERT/Electra by Google, and DeBERTa by Microsoft. There are many, many more and I don't want to confuse you. All you need to know is LLMs are like the guts, or heart and soul of the AI system. By the way, if technical people heard me using the term "AI System", they'd revoke my certifications. I'm just using that so you know when I'm referring to the entire AI ecosystem.

Generative AI: A specific tool inside that toolbox, like a 3D printer. It's a specialized, and advanced tool that can do things like designing and creating content, learning from data to generate cool output and more.

Instructions: This is plain language text that tells the AI system how to behave. Whichever AI system you're using will accept some type of instructions that help it formulate answers when you ask it to do things. This sets a baseline for how it'll respond, but every time you prompt it, it will adjust itself. You can also prompt it with new instructions anytime during your conversation and ask it to recreate previous answers with new instructions.

Prompts: These are different than instructions. Prompts are the statements you give to the AI system. Think of prompts as pieces of code, but without all the annoying syntax. You simply prompt your AI system using normal, everyday language, and it'll respond.

Bots: Bots are like little widgets that serve a specific purpose. There are tens of thousands of Custom GPT bots at chat.openai.com. These can be 'closed bots', meaning you decide what data they use, or open bots that can search the internet, create images and more.

Here's an example, when you hear "AI", you probably hear "Chat GPT". Chat GPT is a product created by Open AI and while it's not the first AI created, at the time of writing this book, it is far and away the most popular.

Chat GPT is based upon Open AI's GPT-4 architecture, which stands for "Generative Pre-trained Transformer 4." GPT-4 is a large language model. You can create a set of instructions and give it to Chat-GPT.

An example of an instruction

"I'm a change manager. I work in a large organization on technology projects but I am not technical. I would like your responses to be simple, and void of 'techno-mumbo-jumbo'. I only need to understand enough to be able to work on these projects"

Once you've added the instructions, you don't have to keep telling the AI system how to respond. If you want it to respond differently, you simply give it different instructions.

An example of a prompt

"I am going to upload a copy of my project charter. I would like you to create 3 different communications. 1) targeted at sponsors and include a high level overview 2) targeted at technical people and include what products and services are affected and 3) targeted at business users who are not technical, but will be using the software when it's launched. Do you need any more context or information to do this?"

Yes, with prompts, you can simply ask the AI what else it might need. For example, one of my kids was designing a video game character and felt stuck. Here's our first prompt:

I am looking to create a character for a story. what are some classic literature examples that can give me ideas for creating a character. what else would you need to know to suggest class literature stories I could read?

GPT-4's response:

～

```
Creating a character for a story is an exciting
process,  and  classic  literature  can  certainly
```

provide a wealth of inspiration. To suggest specific stories or characters from classic literature, it would be helpful to know more about the type of character you're interested in creating. Here are a few questions that could guide my suggestions:

1. Genre Preferences: Are you looking for inspiration from a specific genre, such as romance, adventure, mystery, or fantasy?
2. Character Traits: Are you interested in a particular type of character, such as a hero, villain, antihero, or a complex, multi-dimensional character?
3. Setting and Time Period: Do you have a preference for a particular setting or time period, like medieval times, the Victorian era, or the early 20th century?
4. Themes and Conflicts: Are there specific themes or conflicts you want your character to embody or face, such as love, redemption, revenge, or personal growth?
5. Cultural Background: Are you looking for characters from a specific cultural or geographical background?

Based on your preferences, I can suggest characters from classic literature that might inspire you. For example, if you're interested in a tragic hero, you might look at characters like Hamlet from Shakespeare's "Hamlet." If you're interested in a strong female character, Elizabeth Bennet from Jane Austen's "Pride and Prejudice" might be a good model. Let me know your

```
preferences,   and   I'll   tailor   my   suggestions
accordingly!
```

~

Our response:

> *1) doesn't matter 2) protagonist 3) doesn't matter 4) philosophical and psychological themes 5) doesn't matter what other information would be helpful to give you?*

Note that simply by replying with the number of GPT-4's question, it knew what we were talking about. At time of writing, a single conversation in GPT-4 can hold up to 500 messages. Meaning, it will 'stay in context' for a really long conversation so you don't have to keep telling it the same things over and over.

After we replied, GPT gave us a list of books, but I don't need to add those details here I don't think. The point is, if you don't know how to prompt your AI system, ask it!

Throughout this book, I'll mostly use the term AI, unless I'm referring to a specific company, product, or language model.

Now, as a change manager, none of that probably matters to you, unless you're working on an AI strategy. It would be useful to know this stuff at a high level when you are assigned to the AI project a few days before it's supposed to give live so you can go do some change management things.

A prompt for reviewing this book

Once I finished the chapter, until this point, I asked GPT-4 to help make sure it made sense. This is the prompt I used:

Here is my finalized chapter titled "AI 101 for change managers" The goal is to help non-technical change managers understand the basics of AI as they will likely be pushed into working on AI projects, or they'll want to use AI to help them execute change projects. I would like you to analyze the text and let me know if it makes sense, or if there are any errors. The format should be easy to understand, but if you have other questions, let me know. here's the text: <I pasted the full text of this chapter here>

This is how it responded:

∽

Your chapter titled "AI 101 for Change Managers" provides a clear and accessible introduction to AI for non-technical audiences, particularly change managers. The language is straightforward, and the analogies used are effective in conveying the concepts. Here are some observations and suggestions:

I. Clarity and Accuracy:

- The distinctions between AI, automation, LLMs, and generative AI are well articulated. The analogies used (like AI as a toolbox, automation as a hammer, generative AI as a 3D printer) are apt and help demystify these concepts.
- The explanation of instructions and prompts is clear and provides a practical understanding of how to interact with AI systems.

I. Examples and Contextualization:

- The use of the Chat GPT example is excellent. It provides a concrete instance of AI application that most readers can relate to.
- The inclusion of the conversation example with GPT-4 effectively demonstrates how prompts work and the nature of interactions with an AI model.

I. Potential Areas for Enhancement:

- While the section on different LLMs is informative, it might be slightly advanced for readers who are primarily interested in understanding AI from a change management perspective. Consider if this level of detail is necessary for your target audience or if it could be simplified.
- In the "instructions" section, it could be beneficial to clarify that while initial instructions set a baseline for interaction, each subsequent prompt can subtly alter the AI's responses within that context.

I. Overall Structure and Flow:

- The chapter is well-structured, starting from basic definitions and moving towards more complex concepts. The flow seems logical and easy to follow.
- The concluding paragraph nicely ties back to the relevance of this information for change managers, although it might be strengthened by briefly mentioning how AI

can specifically aid in change management
tasks.

I. Technical Corrections:

- The phrase "at the time of writing this" is
  a bit awkward. Consider rephrasing to "As
  of the time of writing this book".
- Ensure the acronym "GPT-4" is consistent
  (there's a typo where it's written as "GPT-
  4").

Overall, the chapter does a good job of demystifying AI for non-technical change managers and
sets a solid foundation for understanding how AI
can be leveraged in their field. The tone is
appropriate, and the content seems well-tailored
to the intended audience.

~

I removed the confusing part where I listed a bunch of LLMs, fixed
the technical corrections and updated the text for explaining
"instructions vs prompts".

Lastly, I thought it would be funny to include what AI thinks AI is.
For this, I used GPT-4 by Open AI and Co-Pilot by Microsoft.

Microsoft Co-Pilot

~

Artificial intelligence (AI) is a branch of
computer science that aims to create machines
that can perform tasks that typically require

human intelligence, such as learning, reasoning, and problem-solving 1. AI is implemented in machines to perform tasks that actually require human intelligence. Some of their primary functions include reasoning, learning, problem-solving, and more 2. AI has the potential to revolutionize change management by providing real-time data of all activities, predicting future events and challenges, and offering measures to fix them 3. AI can help organizations enhance their current products, optimize internal and external operations, liberate workers to be more creative, and help leaders make better decisions 4. However, realizing the potential of AI requires deploying new technologies that have AI capabilities as widely as possible, which can be a hurdle, especially for global companies with hundreds of employees. This is why change management may be the key to successfully leveraging AI in the business world 3. Change management is a set of processes designed to help organizations and individuals successfully implement new initiatives, including launching new AI solutions and managing reorganizations. The goal of change management is to ensure the success of new initiatives by creating a comprehensive plan to launch and track the impact of new technologies 3. By embracing AI strategically, understanding the nuances of its application, and recognizing the value of human expertise, businesses can navigate change management effectively, seize opportunities, and stay ahead in an era of transformative technology.

∽

Open AI (GPT 4)

AI, or Artificial Intelligence, refers to the development of computer systems that can perform tasks typically requiring human intelligence. These tasks include learning from data (machine learning), recognizing patterns, understanding and responding to natural language (natural language processing), solving complex problems, making decisions, and even perceiving the environment (as in computer vision).

AI operates by processing large amounts of data, identifying patterns and insights, and making decisions based on the data it has been trained on. It ranges from basic automation (like chatbots) to more complex applications (like autonomous vehicles). AI systems are designed and trained by humans and are only as good as the data and algorithms they are built upon. They do not possess consciousness or emotions but can mimic certain aspects of human intelligence and behavior.

Similar definitions, yet vastly different responses. Co-Pilot adds some flavour about implementing an AI strategy while GPT-4 simply gave a definition.

Co-Pilot's answer is obviously derived from their Bing search engine as it gives URLs and references to the articles it used. GPT-4 will tell you, if you ask it.

I will say this a million more times in this book, your use of AI will be limited to the data your tool of choice has been trained on, how it's been programmed, what instructions you give it, and how you prompt it.

Clearing Up Misconceptions

I mentioned a few misconceptions in the opening chapter that I've seen change managers post on LinkedIn. Some of those included:

- AI is just a fancy search engine.
- AI can't take MY job.
- AI can't do the work of a real human.
- AI can't replace a Comms person.

Now, look at the interactions earlier in this chapter and compare that to your perception of AI before reading this. Of course, that's provided you read the first chapter and did the homework exercise I suggested!

To be honest, most of the misconceptions I've read on LinkedIn come from most people having no idea what they're talking about. They have looked at AI at a surface level and decided it's just a search engine. As with all new things, the deeper you go, the more you find out that if you want to remain relevant as a change manager, start learning how to use it or you will end up like Cyberdyne Systems Model 101.[1]

So when I see the blatant misleading information, or plagiarized content from people who clearly should know better, I chalk it up to chest-thumping, which is basically all LinkedIn is good for nowadays.

Anyway, to close this chapter off, I'm going to ask GPT-4 what it thinks the most common misconceptions are:

～

Several common misconceptions about AI persist in the public consciousness, often fueled by sensational media portrayals and a lack of clear understanding. Here are some of the most prevalent ones:

1. AI is Omniscient and Infallible: Many people believe that AI systems are flawless and all-knowing. In reality, AI's abilities are limited to what it has been trained on and can be prone to errors, especially in complex or novel situations.

2. AI Can Fully Replicate Human Intelligence: There's a misconception that AI can replicate all aspects of human intelligence. However, while AI excels in pattern recognition, data processing, and specific tasks, it lacks human qualities like emotional intelligence, creativity, and general common sense.

3. AI Will Lead to Massive Job Losses: While AI will certainly transform the job market and may automate certain tasks, it's also likely to create new job categories and enhance many existing jobs rather than simply replacing human workers wholesale.

4. AI Has Consciousness or Sentience: Some people anthropomorphize AI, attributing it with consciousness or emotions. Current AI systems do not possess consciousness; they operate based on algorithms and data, without personal experiences or emotions.

5. AI Can Solve Any Problem: There is an overestimation of AI's capabilities in

solving all kinds of problems. While AI is a powerful tool, its effectiveness depends on the quality of data, the appropriateness of algorithms, and the context of the problem.

6. AI Operates Independently of Humans: Another misconception is that AI works entirely independently. In reality, AI systems are created, trained, and managed by humans, and their outputs often require human interpretation and decision-making.

7. AI is Always Biased: While there are notable instances of AI exhibiting bias, it's not an inherent trait of AI itself but a reflection of biased data or algorithms used by humans. Efforts are being made to make AI more fair and unbiased.

8. AI is a Single, Unified Technology: People often think of AI as a monolithic technology, but it's actually a collection of diverse technologies and techniques, like machine learning, natural language processing, and computer vision, each with its own applications and limitations.

9. AI Will Lead to a "Superintelligence" Takeover: Popular media often depicts AI leading to a superintelligent takeover. This scenario is speculative and not supported by current AI capabilities or research trajectories.

10. All AI is Similar: There's a tendency to assume that all AI systems are similar in capability and function. However, there's a wide range of AI applications from simple

```
automation tools to complex machine
learning models, each with different
capabilities.
```

Understanding these misconceptions is crucial for a realistic and informed perspective on what AI can and cannot do, and how it should be developed and used responsibly.

∽

Tips for learning about AI

These last two chapters were about as simple as I could make them, but you might be craving more. Here some prompts that can help you:

tell me how banks are using AI?

what are the biggest mistakes companies make when they implement an AI strategy?

what other software do you know of that has integrated AI seamlessly?

what's the difference between instructions and prompts?

how is AI different than a traditional search engine like Google or Bing?

teach me the most important aspects of how to prompt you in order to get better results

There are plenty more, but before I close, I'll paste in the results from GPT-4 and Co-Pilot for that last question:

What GPT-4 thinks about prompting

～

Prompting effectively is key to getting the best results from a language model like me. Here are some crucial aspects to consider for crafting effective prompts:

- Be Clear and Specific: Clearly state what you need. Specificity helps in narrowing down the response to your exact requirements. For instance, instead of asking "Tell me about history," ask "Can you provide an overview of the American Civil War?"
- Provide Context: The more relevant information you provide, the more tailored and accurate the response will be. For example, if you're asking for advice on managing a project, mention the type of project, its size, industry, or any specific challenges you're facing.
- Use Direct Questions: Direct questions often yield more focused answers. For example, instead of saying "I'm wondering about the effects of global warming," ask "What are the primary effects of global warming on arctic ecosystems?"
- Specify the Desired Detail Level: Indicate if you want a brief summary, a detailed explanation, or examples. For instance, "Give me a brief overview of quantum

computing" versus "Explain quantum computing in detail, including its principles and applications."

- Indicate the Type of Response Needed: If you require a response in a specific format — like a list, a step-by-step guide, a summary, or in layman's terms — mention that in your prompt.

- Use Keywords Effectively: Including relevant keywords or terms in your prompt can lead to more accurate responses, especially for technical or specialized topics.

- Sequence Your Queries Logically: If you have multiple questions, order them logically. Start with broader questions and then move to more specific ones.

- Clarify the Purpose or Intent: If the request is for a specific purpose like writing, research, or problem-solving, state that. For instance, "I need arguments for a debate on renewable energy vs. fossil fuels."

- Limitations Acknowledgement: Understand the model's limitations — it's not omniscient and is based on information available up to 2023. It's also not a human, so certain types of reasoning, especially emotional or deeply personal insights, might not be as nuanced as a human's.

- Iterative Approach: Sometimes, you might not get the perfect answer on the first try. It's okay to refine your question based on the response you receive.

Remember, the effectiveness of a response is often directly correlated with how well the question or prompt is constructed. Clear, specific, and well-structured prompts tend to yield the most useful and accurate responses.

∼

What Microsoft Co-Pilot thinks about prompting

∼

Great question! Here are some tips to help you prompt me effectively:

- Be clear and specific: Be explicit about the desired response format from me, whether it's a paragraph, step-by-step instructions, or a list. For example, instead of asking "What are some good restaurants in Seattle?", try asking "Can you provide a list of five highly-rated seafood restaurants in Seattle with outdoor seating?"
- Include context: Include relevant context to help me understand your request. For example, if you're planning a trip to Paris, let me know the dates of your trip and what you're interested in seeing and doing.
- Experiment: Don't be afraid to experiment with different prompts to see what works best. Try rephrasing your prompt or adding

```
   more details to see if it improves the
   quality of my response.
 • Use relevant keywords: Use relevant
   keywords in your prompt to help me
   understand what you're looking for. For
   example, if you're looking for information
   about a specific product, include the
   product name in your prompt.
 • Proofread: Always proofread your prompt to
   ensure it is well-structured and free from
   ambiguity. This will help me understand
   your request more accurately.

I hope these tips help you get better results
from me. If you have any more questions, feel
free to ask!
```

Hmm. I know which AI system I'm sticking with but to close this chapter, think of the AI System as your good 'ol buddy Biff. Imagine you're both sitting out on a patio on nice, crisp -20 Canadian-degree evening having a couple pops.

Act natural, talk natural and don't assume that the AI system needs to be talked to like a robot. Once you break that mental barrier, it'll open your mind up to possibilities, much like it did for my buddy Justin, who's the founder of Idealeap and a Lean Change facilitator.

While spitballing ideas for his book (which is hopefully out soon? now? Dude?!?!?), I gave him an example of what GPT-4 could do and how it could help. He thought of AI largely as a search engine, with robotic and uninteresting responses. I sent him a sample, including the prompts I used and here's how he replied:

Holy shit - your prompts are crazy - I never knew you could prompt to that level!

CHAPTER 5
AI: THE MAJOR PLAYERS

At the time of writing this book, there are three main players in the AI space. Yes, there are more but I imagine if you're a change manager doing some AI things, it's going to involve the technology of one of these three.

Open AI

OpenAI, an artificial intelligence research laboratory, was founded in December 2015 with the mission to ensure that artificial general intelligence (AGI) benefits all of humanity. The company was established as a non-profit organization by a group of prominent individuals in technology and business, including Elon Musk, Sam Altman, Greg Brockman, Ilya Sutskever, Wojciech Zaremba, and John Schulman.

OpenAI's early focus was on conducting research and promoting and developing friendly AI in a way that widely benefits humanity. In its initial years, OpenAI made significant contributions to the field of AI through research and the development of various AI models and technologies. Notably, it focused on ensuring ethical use and equitable access to AI technologies.

In 2019, OpenAI transitioned from a non-profit to a "capped-profit" model with the creation of OpenAI LP, a limited partnership subsidiary. This move was aimed at attracting external investment while still adhering to their fundamental principles. Microsoft became a significant investor and partner, providing funding and computing resources that greatly accelerated OpenAI's research and development capabilities.

OpenAI is widely known for its groundbreaking work in the field of natural language processing. The GPT (Generative Pre-trained Transformer) series, including GPT-3 and the more advanced GPT-4, are among its most notable achievements. These large language models have set new standards in the AI field for their ability to understand and generate human-like text, revolutionizing various applications from automated customer service to content creation.

Throughout its evolution, OpenAI has maintained a commitment to ethical AI development, with a focus on safety, transparency, and broad benefit. It continues to be a leading player in AI research, pushing the boundaries of what's possible in the realm of machine intelligence.

Imagine that, Chat-GPT is all the rage nowadays and it's taking almost a decade to get there.

As I mentioned earlier, they're more commonly known as Chat GPT. Chat GPT is like Kleenex. Nobody calls "facial tissue", facial tissue, they call it Kleenex no matter the brand. Open AI has a variety of products, one of which is Chat GPT.

- Chat GPT itself has a variety of versions (GPT 3, 3.5, 4 and smatterings of sub-versions). As of version 4, which is for paid subscribers only, the dataset is current to April 2023 and you can create images through Dall-E.
- Custom GPTs: This product allows non-technical users to create their own bot and within the next few days as of the

time of writing this book, (January 2024) you'll be able to deploy them into the GPT Store.

- Assistants API: This is a product for developers, although if you're mildly technical, you can use no-code tools to build something neat pretty easily.

Pros: ChatGPT and CustomGPTs can be used by anyone and there are over a thousand plugins available. There is no barrier, other than paying USD $20/month for GPT plug to access GPT-4! It is extremely simple to use for non-technical people.

Cons: The ecosystem evolves so fast that if you plan to build stuff with it, expect out-of-date specs, confusing user support forum topics with outdated information, and implementation docs that might not be all that useful. But of course, you can ask the bot to build the bot for you so maybe that isn't a problem.

Microsoft Co-Pilot

Microsoft is taking an all-in strategy with AI. They're integrating into all of the product suites from Office 365 to Dynamics and more.

- PowerApps/Power Automate: This is essentially Microsoft's no/low-code solution and sorry Microsoft fans, it's utterly terrible compared to platforms like Bubble, Buildbox, Tuddle and more. Don't worry if you don't know what that means.
- Co-Pilot with Bing: This adds AI capability to Microsoft's search engine Bing.
- Co-Pilot with Office 365: Far and away the most useful, and probably most used. This allows you to do neat things with their Office suite. An example would be obviously making summaries of Word docs, taking meeting notes and drafting summaries from One Note .

- Co-Pilot with <insert Microsoft produce here>: yes, there's a Co-Pilot for each product.

Pros: I guess if you're in an enterprise organization using all MS products, it'll be simple to start using it provided your organization pays for it. The pricing varies per product. For example, it's bundled with Windows 11 for free, but costs $30 per user for Office 365.

Cons: As usual with Microsoft, their ecosystem is complicated because each product division implements it in their product. That's why if you, oddly enough, google 'microsoft Co-Pilot', you will find the list of Co-Pilot for <insert product> along with a shit ton of documentation. That means the barrier is higher just because it's more confusing.

Google AI

I have a bone to pick with Google. Here in Canada, the government, in its divine wisdom, laid down an ultimatum to Big Tech to make them pay for news sourced in Canada. So Big Tech essentially gave Canada the middle finger and excluded all Canadian media outlets as sources of data.

That means Google Bard (as of January 2024) is available in over 30 countries and Canada isn't one of them. Their official stance is "due to regulatory uncertainty" but we all know how big business works. Mess with me, we mess right back and Google doesn't need Canada for anything so they automatically win. That's why I'm not including any Google examples in this book, simply because I can't use it without some workarounds.

Here's what GPT-4 thinks about Google's AI ecosystem:

~

Google's AI ecosystem is a comprehensive and integrated suite of technologies, platforms, and services that leverage artificial intelligence to provide various solutions and capabilities. Key components of Google's AI ecosystem include:

- Google AI: This is Google's overarching division dedicated to AI research and development. It focuses on advancing the state of the art in AI through research and applying AI to products and new domains.
- TensorFlow: An open-source machine learning framework developed by Google Brain. TensorFlow is widely used for creating machine learning and neural network models, particularly deep learning models.
- Google Cloud AI: A suite of cloud-based AI services and tools offered through Google Cloud Platform (GCP). This includes APIs for natural language processing, translation, vision recognition, and conversation AI, as well as AutoML services for training custom models with minimal machine learning expertise.
- DeepMind: A subsidiary of Alphabet Inc. (Google's parent company), DeepMind is a research lab renowned for its work in deep learning and artificial general intelligence. DeepMind has made significant advancements in AI, notably in developing AI systems capable of mastering complex games like Go and chess.
- Google Assistant: Google's AI-powered virtual assistant, available on various devices, uses natural language processing

and machine learning to understand and respond to user queries.

- BERT and Other Language Models: Google has developed several advanced language processing models, such as BERT (Bidirectional Encoder Representations from Transformers), which significantly improve the understanding of user queries in its search engine.
- AI for Social Good: Google AI is involved in projects and initiatives that apply AI to societal challenges, including environmental conservation, healthcare, and education.
- Research and Publications: Google AI researchers regularly publish papers and contribute to the broader academic and research community, driving forward the field of AI.
- AI Ethics and Principles: Google has established a set of AI principles to guide its ethical development and use of artificial intelligence.
- AI Tools for Developers: Google offers various tools and platforms, like ML Kit for mobile developers and Colab for AI research prototyping, making AI more accessible to a broader range of developers.

Google's AI ecosystem is characterized by its depth, diversity, and commitment to both advancing AI technology and applying it in practical, ethical, and socially beneficial ways.

The purpose of this chapter is to help point you to the most common AI ecosystems as I imagine if you're getting involved in technology projects, it'll be with one of these three.

Now, if you are reading this book because you want to use AI to help with change management and aren't necessarily working on a technology project, I highly recommend paying the $20 a month for GPT Plus.

While writing this book I was flipping between GPT-3, GPT-4 and Co-Pilot, plus using a variety of SasS tools that have integrated AI into their products and GPT-4 is far and away the most useful. The only problem being the data GPT-4 is trained on is only current to April 2023.

All AIs are Not Created Equally!

I mentioned this a few times in the last chapter, whatever AI system you use is only as good as the data it uses, how it was trained, the algorithms it uses and the instructions, and prompts, you feed it.

Here's a perfect example. Yesterday I asked Co-Pilot the same questions as GPT-4 to compare the output for this book. One of Co-Pilot's responses specifically recommended Microsoft's products whereas GPT-4 did not. I will go into more details about the ethics of this later.

Today I wanted to go back to those chats and with GPT-4, it's simple. Go to chat.openai.com and you'll see a list of all of your chats. Go to Co-Pilot and you have to jump through typical Microsoft hoops just to find your history. The instructions say to go to Bing.com and click the 'show all recent chats' button.

There is no such button.

So I asked Co-Pilot to find them and it couldn't. Delightful. Serves me right for closing my browser. Anyway, I started over again and asked both GPT-4 and Co-Pilot what they have been trained on.

What GPT-4 thinks AI is

~

AI, or Artificial Intelligence, is a broad term that encompasses any computer system designed to perform tasks that normally require human intelligence. This includes a wide range of capabilities such as recognizing speech, learning, planning, problem-solving, perception, and even the ability to move or manipulate objects. AI systems can range from simple, rule-based algorithms to complex, self-learning systems based on machine learning and neural networks.

Large Language Models (LLMs), like the one you're interacting with now, are a specific type of AI. They are sophisticated models designed to understand, generate, and interpret human language. Here are some key characteristics of LLMs:

1. Trained on Extensive Text Data: LLMs are trained on vast amounts of text data, which enables them to understand and generate language in a way that's coherent and contextually relevant.
2. Ability to Generate Text: One of the primary functions of LLMs is generating text. This can be used for a variety of applications, from answering questions to creating content.

3. Understanding Context and Nuances: LLMs are designed to understand context, nuances, and even the subtleties of language, such as sarcasm, humor, or cultural references.
4. Machine Learning Based: These models use machine learning, especially deep learning techniques, to continuously improve their language processing capabilities.

In summary, while all large language models are a form of AI, not all AI systems are large language models. LLMs are specialized AI tools focused on language-related tasks, whereas AI can encompass a much broader range of capabilities beyond just language processing.

∿

What Microsoft Co-Pilot thinks AI is

∿

As an AI conversational agent, I do not have a single knowledge base. Instead, I use a variety of technologies, including deep learning frameworks such as TensorFlow, PyTorch, and Keras, as well as natural language processing (NLP) and computer vision1.

When you ask me a question, I analyze the text to understand the meaning behind your words. I then use my knowledge base and internal tools to generate a response that is relevant to your question. My responses are designed to be helpful, positive, polite, empathetic, interesting, entertaining, and engaging.

Is there anything else I can help you with?

$\sim$

I asked Co-Pilot to explain how it derives its responses and it gave me the same answer. Then after five prompts, yes five prompts, it told me I needed to start a new conversation because I had reached the limit.

Now, yesterday when I asked this same question, Co-Pilot's answer was completely different. It gave a similar response to GPT-4, but went on to say how to use Microsoft's BI tools and Power Apps to do certain things.

This is perhaps another gigantic lesson when you're going to be tasked with implementing an AI strategy, or when working on AI implementation projects. You are never going to get repeatable results, even by using the exact same prompt. As the AI learns, its answers evolve and that might be problematic for some.

The other lesson might be, if you're forced into a project that uses Microsoft's AI products, it's going to be much more complicated. Given the quality of the responses I've compared for this book, Co-Pilot has a long road ahead of it. Plus, with Microsoft's typically siloed approach to product development, it'll be much more complicated and probably frustrating to deal with.

But don't take my word for it, head over to Reddit and see what people think of it.

CHAPTER 6

CHANGE MANAGEMENT BEFORE AI

How many times have you worked on a change project and found the
documentation to be out of date?
How many communications have you sent out that no one read?
How many times have you repeated yourself?
How many times did you create and re-create training materials?
How many times have you repeated yourself?

T hink of this chapter as the most basic introduction to what
change management is and what the most common challenges we face. It's impossible to cover it all in one chapter
but I thought it was important to look at what change management
typically looks like in a non-AI world and then compare it to what it
can look like in an AI world. If you're a seasoned change manager,
hopefully you're seasoned with a little salt, onion powder, garlic
powder and some mix of aromatics.

Sorry if that sounded creepy, I was poking fun at people who actually
put "seasoned <whatever title they want>" on their LinkedIn profiles.

What I meant was, if you're an experienced change manager, you can
probably skip this chapter, it's just for setting context so I can do

some comparisons about how these things will change as a result of AI.

So to make it easy on myself, I'll use Open AI to help describe the three main components of change management:

1. Two main types of change initiatives
2. A general process for managing change
3. The main roles and responsibilities of the people tasked with implementing the change

~

Two Types of Change Initiatives

The two big buckets are project-based change management and transformation-based change management:

Project-Based Change Management:

- Focus and Scope: This approach is typically focused on specific, well-defined changes with a clear start and end point. These changes are often related to implementing new systems, processes, or structures within the organization.
- Nature of Change: The changes are usually incremental and can be isolated to certain departments or functions. They do not generally impact the entire organization.
- Management Approach: Project-based change is managed using traditional project management tools and techniques. It involves detailed planning, clear

objectives, resource allocation, and timeline management.

- Stakeholder Involvement: Involvement is often limited to those directly affected by the change or those who are needed to implement it. The focus is on managing the transition for these specific groups.
- Measurement of Success: Success is measured against predefined objectives and timelines, such as on-time and on-budget delivery, and achievement of specific project goals.

Transformation-Based Change Management:

- Focus and Scope: This approach deals with wide-ranging, fundamental changes that affect the entire organization. These changes are often driven by a need to adapt to significant external shifts, like market changes, technological advancements, or cultural shifts.
- Nature of Change: The changes are comprehensive and deeply affect the organization's strategy, culture, and operations. They are transformational rather than incremental.
- Management Approach: Transformation-based change requires a more holistic and flexible approach. It involves strategic visioning, cultural alignment, leadership commitment, and an ongoing process of engagement and communication across all levels of the organization.

- Stakeholder Involvement: It requires broad involvement and buy-in from stakeholders at all levels. The focus is on shifting mindsets, behaviors, and organizational culture.
- Measurement of Success: Success is measured not just in terms of specific objectives but also in the overall shift in organizational performance and culture. It's often evaluated over a longer period.

You could say that project-based change management is more tactical while transformation-based change management is strategic, albeit mostly run like a project, which always works, right?

A project-based change might be changing the technology for how you're building engines for an airplane.

A transformational-based change might be figuring out how to change the engine of the plane while it's in the air.

The general process for managing changes.

For the record, I don't believe in step-based change management[1]. It doesn't work and it doesn't make any sense to follows steps and phases for complex change.

That being said, google 'change management process' and you'll see hundreds of thousands of diagrams and tried-and-true methods/frameworks/models that are more or less the same:

1. Identify the need for change.
2. Craft a change strategy.
3. Assess/Analyze the current state.

4. Create the plan.
5. Execute the plan.
6. Lessons learned.

And, again, because this a book about AI, here's what Open AI had to say:

∼

Managing a change project typically involves several key steps, each crucial for ensuring that the change is effectively implemented and embraced within an organization. Here's a general outline of these steps:

Identify the Need for Change:

- Recognize the factors driving the need for change, whether they are internal or external. This could be due to market shifts, internal challenges, technological advancements, or other factors.

Define Clear Objectives and Scope:

- Clearly define what the change project aims to achieve. Set specific, measurable, achievable, relevant, and time-bound (SMART) objectives.

Develop a Change Management Plan:

- This plan should outline the approach for managing the change, including strategies for communication, stakeholder engagement, training, and support.

Assess Change Impact and Stakeholder Analysis:

- Analyze how the change will impact different parts of the organization and identify key stakeholders. Understand stakeholder attitudes towards the change and plan accordingly.

Communication and Engagement:

- Develop a communication strategy to keep stakeholders informed and engaged throughout the change process. Effective communication is critical for building support and minimizing resistance.

Provide Training and Support:

- Equip employees with the necessary skills and knowledge to handle the change. This may involve training programs, workshops, or one-on-one support sessions.

Implement the Change:

- Execute the change according to the plan. This may involve a phased approach, starting with a pilot or gradual implementation before full-scale execution.

Monitor and Manage Resistance:

- Be vigilant for signs of resistance and manage them proactively. Address concerns and provide support to those struggling with the change.

Track Progress and Measure Success:

- Use predefined metrics to monitor the progress of the change initiative. Evaluate the success of the project against the initial objectives set.

Review and Adapt:

- Continuously review the impact of the change and be ready to adapt the approach if necessary. Gather feedback and make adjustments to support the ongoing success of the change initiative.

Reinforce and Institutionalize the Change:

- Ensure that the change is embedded in the culture and processes of the organization. This may involve updating policies, procedures, and reinforcing the change through ongoing communication and training.

These steps are not necessarily linear and may overlap or require revisiting as the change project progresses. The key is to be flexible and responsive to the needs and reactions of the organization and its stakeholders.

~

For the record, I don't agree with any of that. Remember GPT-4 is just using the data it's been trained on and that nonsense above is plastered all over the internet.

Roles and Responsibilities

I'll focus on the holy trinity: Change Manager, Project Manager, and the Comms person. Yes, more people might be involved, but I want to keep it simple. Since the day will never come when the change management world understands that separating these roles is by far the stupidest thing to do, let's see what insights Open AI can give us about the differences between them.

~

Change Manager:

- Focus: The primary focus of a Change Manager is to manage the human aspects of change. This includes preparing, supporting, and helping individuals, teams, and organizations in making organizational change.
- Responsibilities:
- Developing and implementing change management strategies and plans that maximize employee adoption and minimize resistance.
- Assessing the change impact and organizational readiness for change.
- Engaging and communicating with stakeholders across all levels of the organization to facilitate the change process.

- Providing support and guidance to all levels of management and supervisors as they help their direct reports through transitions.
- Identifying and managing anticipated resistance to change.
- Collaborating with project teams to integrate change management activities into the overall project plan.
- Measuring and monitoring the effectiveness of change initiatives, ensuring alignment with strategic objectives.

Project Manager:

- Focus: A Project Manager focuses on the planning, executing, monitoring, controlling, and closing of projects. They are responsible for ensuring that projects are completed on time, within budget, and within scope.

Responsibilities:

- Defining the project scope and objectives, involving all relevant stakeholders and ensuring technical feasibility.
- Developing a detailed project plan to track progress and manage project resources.
- Managing changes to the project scope, schedule, and costs using appropriate verification techniques.
- Measuring project performance using appropriate tools and techniques.

- Managing the relationship with the client and all stakeholders, ensuring the project meets their expectations.
- Identifying and mitigating risks and issues throughout the project lifecycle.
- Creating and maintaining comprehensive project documentation.

Oh, and I guess the 3rd role is the comms person. You know, they're the person the writes the emails and newsletters and stuff.

Most Common Challenges

Since 2014, I've been collecting change challenges from all over the world and most recently through a free, open-sourced 'State of Change Management[2]' survey Gilbert Kruidenier and I started in 2018. I have read plenty of "State of" reports from Version One's State of Agile surveys to plenty of others that try to uncover what's working and not working in change.

The insights are more or less always the same:

- Change fails because we struggle to get a seat at the table.
- Leaders involve us too late.
- We're forced to follow archaic processes.
- We can't get buy-in.
- People are resisting.

This is how Open AI summarized the "State of Change Management" answers from 75 change managers (at the time of writing this) when asked what their toughest challenges were:

1. Leadership and Ownership Challenges: A significant number of responses point to difficulties in securing leadership buy-in, sponsorship, and engagement. Challenges like "Leadership disengagement," "Getting time with sponsor," and "Sponsors and senior leaders owning the change" highlight that a common obstacle is the lack of active and visible support from those at the top.

2. Cultural Resistance and Organizational Dynamics: Resistance to change due to organizational culture is another prevalent theme. Terms such as "Organizational culture," "Company culture and resistance to change," and "Working as a change manager on projects, knowing that the organization will revert back to its cultural norms" suggest that entrenched ways of working and thinking are significant barriers to change.

3. Change Implementation and Adaptation Issues: Many responses illustrate the struggle with the practical aspects of implementing change. This includes "navigating different perspectives," "Balancing big picture with attention to detail," and "Managing change in a complex, fast-moving environment." The need to adapt change practices to diverse environments, overcome resistance, and address the pace of change are key challenges.

≈

The point is, it could be the year 2084 when you're reading this and I guarantee these patterns will be same. Well, that's provided AI didn't take all the change management jobs. If it did and you're a robot analyzing this text, I wonder what you'd think?

What's the Point?

The point is, the pre-AI change management world is predicated on industrial thinking. Change can be ensured by following the proper standardized steps, there is clear delineation between the roles on a change project and there are distinct strategies and approaches for project-based, or transformational change.

We know change has always been dynamic but there was a point in time where you could have a five person change team, much like my five person web team. You had the luxury of making big plans and documents created through extremely long planning cycles.

That world doesn't exist anymore, well, maybe if you work in a bank, telecom or insurance where change initiatives are mostly an exercise in change theatre, but for real, deep, meaningful change, we need to change how we do change.

Now let's switch gears and look at what change management will be (is?) like in a post-AI world. But before that, let's see what Open AI thought about this closing paragraph.

My Prompt:

> I am writing a book about how AI will change change management. This is the end of chapter where I describe why traditional change management will become obsolete and traditional change management roles will transform. I am going to paste the text here and would like you to analyze if the closing of the chapter makes sense. I'd also like you to suggest ideas for improving it.

GPT-4

∼

Your closing remarks in the chapter effectively highlight the contrast between traditional change management and the emerging requirements in an AI-driven era. The text captures the essence of how AI is transforming the landscape of change management, moving away from rigid, industrial-era methodologies to more dynamic, responsive approaches. Here are some suggestions and points for consideration to enhance the closing of your chapter:

- Illustrate with Examples: Provide concrete examples or case studies of how AI has already begun transforming change management in certain industries. This could help readers visualize the practical implications of your argument.
- Address Skepticism: Acknowledge potential skepticism from traditionalists in change management. Discussing common counterarguments to your thesis and providing reasoned responses could strengthen your position.
- Discuss the Role of AI in Change Management: Elaborate on how AI specifically contributes to this transformation. For instance, AI's role in predictive analysis, real-time feedback, personalized communication strategies, or automated routine tasks could be highlighted.
- Future of Change Management Roles: Expand on how traditional roles in change

management might evolve. What new skills
will be required? How will the focus of
these roles shift? This can give a clearer
picture of the future you envisage.

- Impact on Strategy and Planning: Discuss
  how AI affects the strategic planning
  aspect of change management. How does AI
  change the way strategies are formulated
  and executed?
- Ethical and Cultural Considerations:
  Briefly touch upon any ethical
  considerations and cultural shifts within
  organizations that might arise due to the
  integration of AI in change management.
- Concluding Statement: End with a strong,
  forward-looking statement that encapsulates
  the core message of your chapter and sets
  the stage for what's coming next in your
  book. This could be a reflection on the
  potential of AI to revolutionize change
  management or a call to action for
  embracing these changes.

Overall, your chapter ending effectively sets the
tone for a shift towards a more AI-integrated
approach in change management. Enhancing it with
the above elements could provide a more rounded
perspective and a stronger closing argument.

For the record, that's precisely what my plan was for the upcoming
chapters. Let's dig in, shall we?

CHAPTER 7

CHANGE MANAGEMENT AFTER AI

Being the astute reader you are, you're probably wondering why the last chapter was "Change Management Before AI" and this chapter is "Change Management After AI". It implies there is some flip of the switch into this new modern world.

But there isn't. In this chapter, I'm going to show you ideas for how AI can help you with six things:

1. Designing Training Sessions.
2. Data Analysis.
3. Communications.
4. Project/Change Management Assistance.
5. Better Meetings.
6. Content Creation.

I'm going to toss out a few examples here and to be clear, I am writing all of these prompts and ideas for Open AI's GPT-4. That means when I say:

- Ask AI to: I mean, go to chat.openai.com and use that prompt.
- Go back to the same thread: I mean go to chat.openai.com and select the chat you already created.

These aren't independent things, meaning there is some overlap. For example, you'd use some type of data analysis in all of these six buckets. I'll keep this chapter about ideas and possibilities and in the final section of the book show you the actual prompts you can use and what data you'd need, and how you would need to format that data to make it work. But first, let's talk about how to start making the shift to using AI.

The shift to using AI will be a nightmare. An absolute nightmare, and here's why:

- Companies are not ready for it, and simply can't be ready for it in the traditional sense. more on that later.
- The technology evolves so rapidly that in certain cases, AI may give you unpredictable results as it evolves and learns more.
- Companies will just want to do AI stuff to avoid being left behind, meaning there's no intention or purpose.
- Companies who like to plan things will never start because the technology changes too fast. That will make people leave for organizations that are on the cutting edge.

This is going to make it tough on the change managers.

To be more specific about using AI in change management, that might not be as bad. The biggest challenge will be overcoming the desire to control what the AI is doing, which sort of defeats the purpose of using it.

Spoiler Alert: Imagine you've implemented an AI-based project status repository, which I'll show you how to do later. Imagine after some months of use, and training some stakeholder gets a slightly different answer than what they did a few weeks earlier?

> Remember, AI continually learns from its interactions. Generally speaking, the answer would be reasonably similar each time you ask it the same question, there's a change it could be different if it was re-trained on new data between questions. This will be, by far, the biggest barrier to AI adoption in change management because that is a gigantic risk.

Sounds crazy, but some people cling to stability and predictability and all I can say is, I ran hundreds of tests on prompts while writing this book. As I interacted with the AI system, it learned and the answer changed a little. The intent and main points weren't changed, but still, different is different.

When you think of how most organizations change and how long it takes most organizations to adopt new technology or ideas, there's a good chance the AI landscape will look completely different even weeks after considering using it.

Look how long it took for Agile to become mainstream. I started helping organizations make the shift in the early 2000s and here we are, a quarter of decade later, and most people still think it's just a process that makes things go faster. I am NOT going down this rabbit hole.

Before I get Open AI to help out with what change management will look like in an AI world, here's a bit of an expansion of the things I mentioned in the first chapter. I'm going to reduce these points to things that would be useful in change management because I use AI for everything from helping write code, to graphic creation, research and more.

Customized, and personalized messaging: I've fed a 'standard comms' into Open AI, prompted it with the parameters of the change project along with personas of the people involved and asked it to create a version of the comms that are individualized for those personas.

Presentation Creation: Everyone who likes creating 'decks', raise your hands! I've used AI to create the foundational structure for everything from pitch decks for the startup I'm working for, to product overview and updates for customers.

Transcription Creation, Translation, Speech-to-text and vice-versa: Whenever I do a webinar or training, people want the recording but no one watches it. I use AI to create a searchable webinar complete with links to the timestamps. This way people can ask about a topic and be directed to the part of the video that has the relevant discussion.

Help and project documentation via chat bots: Help documentation is important but instead of trying to categorize and tag things properly, I use a custom AI bot that lets users ask a question and the responses are created dynamically from my help documents.

Imagine feeding your bot all of your project charters, RACI matrices, status reports and more and letting people just ask things like:

- Who's responsible for the implementation of system X?
- Analyze the last 5 status reports and point out any inconsistencies or risks we might want to be looking at.

Real-time data analysis: I mentioned that State of Change management report earlier, that's all automated. As people fill out the survey, the bot is updated automatically so if you asked it a year ago what change managers are most existed to learn about and then asked it today, you'd get different answers.

To me, this last point is the one that'll have the greatest impact.

AI has the ability to help you make sense of large data sets extremely quickly so you can make more well informed decisions faster.

The best part is, you can control the data. Well, that's the theoretical best part, but in a future chapter I'll look at the ethical problem that creates.

Ok, now let's explore how AI thinks AI will change change management

~

AI can significantly impact and improve change management in various ways:

- Predictive Analysis and Planning: AI can predict potential challenges and outcomes of change initiatives by analyzing data trends. This helps in devising more effective strategies and reduces risks associated with changes.
- Personalized Communication: AI can tailor communication regarding change initiatives to various stakeholders. By understanding individual preferences and resistance points, it can help in crafting messages that are more likely to be well-received and understood.
- Real-Time Feedback and Adaptation: With AI, organizations can collect and analyze feedback in real-time, allowing them to adapt their strategies quickly. This agility is crucial in ensuring the success of change management as conditions and perceptions evolve.
- Enhanced Decision-Making: AI can provide decision-makers with insights derived from large data sets, helping to inform and

enhance the decision-making process. It can identify unseen patterns and make recommendations, leading to more informed and strategic decisions.

- Automation of Routine Tasks: By automating routine and administrative tasks, AI frees up human resources to focus on more strategic aspects of change management, such as stakeholder engagement and leadership.
- Training and Development: AI can be used to create personalized training programs for employees to help them adapt to change. It can identify skill gaps and recommend courses, ensuring that the workforce is well-prepared.
- Resistance Management: AI can help in identifying resistance patterns and sources among employees. By analyzing behaviors and feedback, AI can suggest targeted interventions to manage and mitigate resistance effectively.
- Cultural Insights: AI can analyze organizational culture and employee sentiments, providing insights into how changes might impact the work environment. This helps in aligning change initiatives with the organizational culture or in preparing strategies to shift the culture if needed.

By leveraging these capabilities, AI can make change management more strategic, responsive, and effective, ultimately leading to higher success rates in organizational change initiatives.

~

There are some interesting points here, but remember, AI is only as good as the data it's been trained on. So I asked it:

earlier in this thread I asked you: "how can ai impact and improve change management?" where did you get the data for that response and how did you summarize it like that?

~

The response I provided earlier about how AI can impact and improve change management was not based on data from a specific source. Instead, it was synthesized from my training data, which includes a wide array of texts up to my last update in April 2023. This training involves extensive information on topics such as AI, change management, organizational behavior, and technology trends.

When summarizing information like this, I draw upon the general principles and examples commonly discussed in the field of AI and change management. The aim is to provide a comprehensive and accurate overview that aligns with current knowledge and practices in these areas. However, it's important to note that the response is a synthesis of generally known information and does not cite specific studies or sources. For the most current research or case studies, consulting the latest literature in the field would be advisable.

～

That seemed a little generic, so I asked it again and this time it expanded a bit more:

～

The response to your question about how AI can impact and improve change management was based on my training data, which includes a wide range of sources up until April 2023. This data encompasses books, articles, academic research, and other educational materials that cover topics related to AI, change management, and their intersection.

To summarize the information, I followed these steps:

- Identifying Relevant Concepts: I identified key areas where AI can impact change management, such as predictive analysis, personalized communication, and decision-making.
- Synthesizing Information: I synthesized information from various sources to create a comprehensive overview. This involves integrating ideas and examples that are commonly discussed in the context of AI and change management.
- Simplifying for Clarity: I aimed to present the information in a clear, concise manner

suitable for a broad audience, avoiding overly technical jargon.

- Ensuring Relevance and Accuracy: I focused on including information that is relevant and reflects current understanding and practices in the field.
- Structuring the Response: The response was structured to provide a clear, logical flow of how AI impacts different facets of change management.

It's important to note that while I strive for accuracy and relevance, the information provided is a general overview and might not capture the most recent developments or specific case studies in the field post-April 2023.

I'm going to close off this chapter with digging further into how AI things AI will evolve to help change managers in the next 5 years. I asked:

> a chapter of my book is about what change management was like before AI and what it's like now by using AI. I used some of your responses from my previous questions. I want to ask you based on understanding how AI can help change management and understanding how it worked before AI, can you make predictions about how AI will evolve in the next 5 years to help change managers?

Predicting how AI will evolve in the next five years to aid change management involves considering current trends and potential advancements in technology. Based on the understanding of AI's current capabilities and its impact on change management, here are some predictions:

- Enhanced Predictive Analytics: AI will likely become more sophisticated in predicting the outcomes and potential obstacles of change initiatives. By analyzing vast datasets, AI could provide more accurate forecasts, helping change managers anticipate challenges and plan more effectively.
- Improved Personalization in Change Processes: As AI becomes more adept at understanding individual behaviors and preferences, change managers could use AI to tailor communication and training more effectively. This personalization will increase the likelihood of successful change adoption at an individual level.
- Automated Monitoring and Adaptation: AI systems could evolve to monitor the progress of change initiatives in real-time, providing instant feedback and suggestions for course correction. This could lead to more dynamic and responsive change management strategies.
- Advanced Decision Support Systems: AI could offer more nuanced and complex decision-making support, analyzing scenarios and providing recommendations that account for a wide range of variables, including human factors, economic impacts, and long-term strategic alignment.

- Integration with Virtual and Augmented Reality: For training and simulation purposes, AI could integrate with VR and AR technologies to create immersive learning environments. This could be particularly useful in preparing employees for complex changes in their work processes or environment.
- Enhanced Change Impact Analysis: AI might be able to conduct deeper and more nuanced impact analyses of proposed changes, considering factors like employee morale, cultural fit, and potential ripple effects across the organization.
- Robotic Process Automation (RPA) in Routine Change Management Tasks: AI-driven automation could handle routine tasks in change management, such as updating project documents, scheduling meetings, or collating feedback, freeing up human managers to focus on more strategic aspects.
- Emotion AI for Gauging Employee Sentiment: Advances in emotion AI could enable more accurate assessments of employee sentiments towards change, allowing change managers to address concerns and resistance more effectively.
- AI-driven Collaboration Tools: Enhanced AI tools could facilitate better collaboration among teams, especially in remote or distributed work environments, ensuring that change initiatives are cohesively implemented.

- Ethical and Responsible AI Use: As AI
  becomes more integral to change management,
  there will likely be a greater emphasis on
  ethical AI practices, ensuring
  transparency, fairness, and respect for
  privacy in how AI is employed.

These predictions are speculative and based on
the current trajectory of AI development and its
application in change management. The actual
evolution of AI will depend on various factors,
including technological breakthroughs, regulatory
frameworks, and shifts in organizational priorities and practices.

～

You'll notice some of the answers were similar to the first question I asked about how AI will change change management, but there was a little more specificity in the answer.

You might have also noticed this last response was less robotic and tactical and expanded more on human elements like ethics, responsible use and using AI-driven automation to make the project manager obsolete.

Practically, when I think back to all the change related roles I've had, whether that's an agile coach, change manager, product manager or director/leader, this is specifically how AI has shifted how I do change. In the next section, and coming chapters, I'll show you how to feed AI your data, and how to train and prompt it.

For now, here are six practical ways AI can help you in change management.

1. Designing Training Sessions

I'm not sure if this is true for you, but for me, static, pre-planned training sessions don't work. I much prefer to make them dynamic. Even if it's a session for training on a new system I don't like to plan out every detail and blast people with information.

These sessions take time to plan and there are thousands of websites with different activities for ice-breakers, team building, teaching certain topics through play and interaction and more.

While working as an agile coach at a telecom company, we were acting as 'train the trainers', that is, we were training our replacements because consultants are expensive. The people we were training were amazed at how much time and effort went into designing a team liftoff session.

Now the obvious counter-argument is to simply make a playbook and keep doing the same thing for all teams. I don't like playbooks and no team is the same so the experience should be customized to their context. In the last section I'll dig into details, including prompts I use, but for now, here's how AI can save you hours and days of work.

Remember, AI stays in context so you don't have to keep telling it what the session is for.

- Feed it a little context about the team, what the session is for, how long you have and the intent. Ask it generate pre-workshop survey questions.
- Ask it for ice-breaker activities.
- Ask it to create your slides, instructions and 'how to prepare' email.
- Ask it to suggest activities to teach a particular topic.
- If it's training for a new system, upload the entire help file or manuals and ask it to summarize it, create a fun game to teach people the most important bits etc.

2. Data Analysis

This one is where AI shines. While working as a product owner, I stopped using questions with rating systems. These types of survey questions are only used because they're easy to score.

An example might be: How often do you use feature X? Always, seldom, never.

Instead, I ask questions like:

- How does using our software make your job easier?
- What is the most difficult thing to accomplish in our software?
- What would you change about our software if you had a magic wand?

Now to be fair, it's easy to do this now and just look at all the answers. What happens when you have thousands of users? Hundreds of thousands? That breaks quickly. I know who is logged in, so now I can upload the data to an AI bot and ask it:

- How many users have filled out our survey?
- Analyze the responses for the first two questions of the survey and give me a sentiment analysis of what people think about it. Note I said "the first two questions". I don't have to tell it specifically what to get, it'll just grab the first two questions from my data set.
- Compare the survey results to the product feature sheet and tell me which features customer like the most.
- Given what customers have said is difficult, make some suggestions about what we could do to improve those features.

You might thing that's not change management related, but it is. Think about how cutting change records would be if you, or the project manager, needed to create a report to stakeholders. Or, what if there was no project manager and it got dumped on you.

The possibilities with data analysis are endless. Now AI says it can help with change management with predictive analysis of change initiatives. Giant caveat, it can only do that given the data you feed it. Here's what it means by that:

- Data-Driven Predictions: AI algorithms can process vast amounts of historical data to identify patterns and trends that may not be apparent to humans. This includes analyzing past change initiatives, their success rates, challenges encountered, and the factors that influenced their outcomes.
- Scenario Modelling: AI can simulate various scenarios based on different inputs and variables. This helps in understanding the potential impacts of different change strategies and choosing the one with the highest likelihood of success. For example, AI can model how changes in organizational structure or process modifications might affect productivity or employee satisfaction.
- Risk Identification and Mitigation: AI tools can proactively identify potential risks in change initiatives. By analyzing factors such as employee sentiment, market trends, and operational data, AI can highlight areas of concern, allowing managers to address these risks before they become problematic.
- Customized Strategy Development: Based on the predictive analysis, AI can recommend tailored strategies for change management. This can include identifying the most effective communication channels, the best timing for implementing changes, and the right pacing for different phases of the change process.
- Enhanced Decision-Making: With AI's ability to analyze complex data sets, change managers can make more

informed decisions. AI's insights can complement human judgment, leading to more nuanced and effective planning.

- Monitoring and Adjustment: AI doesn't just predict and plan; it can also monitor the progress of change initiatives in real-time. This allows for ongoing adjustments to the strategy, ensuring that the change management process remains aligned with organizational goals and external conditions.

- Stakeholder Analysis: AI can analyze stakeholder data to predict how different groups within the organization might react to the change. Understanding stakeholder attitudes and concerns early in the process can inform more effective stakeholder engagement strategies.

- Predictive Analytics for Training Needs: AI can predict which departments or employees might need additional training or support during the change process, allowing for proactive planning of training programs.

- Forecasting Outcomes: AI can provide forecasts about the outcomes of change initiatives, including potential increases in efficiency, cost savings, and improvements in employee engagement, helping to build a business case for the change.

- Continuous Learning: As AI systems are exposed to more data over time, their predictions and recommendations become more accurate and refined, leading to continuous improvement in change management strategies.

I bet that sounds magical, doesn't it? Again, this chapter is about possibilities, check out the final section of this book to see how you can prompt AI to do this.

3. Communications

This is another obvious one. If you've read any my other work, you'll know I'm a fan of creating meaningful dialogue over broadcasting communications[1], but sometimes blasting out information is necessary.

Here's how AI can help make your communications more efficient:

- **Personalized messaging**: You can ask AI to create as many versions of a communication based on personas. Example: create one for executives in a 'be brief, be bold, be gone' tone and another in a more friendly, informative tone. The obvious criticism of this is that the communications should be standardized because we don't want confusion! Separate the intent and the message from the delivery style. Problem solved.
- **Formatting for Mediums**: You can ask AI to create 'tweet' (yes, I know it's X now) sized nuggets, video scripts, explainer video scripts, blog posts, formal documentation, summaries and more. If you have multiple internal communication channels like slack, discord, or some type of facebook style intranet, AI can make sure the message is appropriate for the medium.
- **Analyzing feedback**: Another obvious one, if your communications involves a survey, or feedback from sticky notes on a wall (or tool), you can feed that into AI and ask it to analyze the sentiment. Spoiler alert, you can take a screenshot of Miro, or any online sticky note tool and AI will read the stickies so you don't need to copy/paste the text.
- **Campaign analysis**: Another obvious one. If you're using some type of newsletter service like Mail Chimp, Active Campaign etc., you can turn AI loose on your reports and ask it to tell you which messages are popular, which links get clicked on, who's reading and not reading them etc. Now, all

newsletter tools have reports, but with AI, you can analyze multiple reports within seconds and find the content and links that are resonating with people.

- **Intelligent Help:** I'll write more about this in the Project and Change Management Assistance section, but imagine a 'ask the help file' widget that lets people ask questions about the change. You can store what questions they ask and simply feed it all of your newsletter campaigns, intranet sites, and docs and let AI respond.

4. Project and Change Management Assistance

I've never understood why the change world puts so much energy into keeping these separate. It's impossible to separate them because it leads to misalignment, frustration, and most importantly, completely inaccurate progress and analysis about how the change is actually going.

There will always be a need to manage administrative things, like the budget, schedule and documents. AI can make this so simple, you might not even need a project manager. And vice versa. You'll just need a T-shaped change person who can do both.

This section could be a book on its own, so I'll summarize what I think are the most important things AI can help with:

- **Real-time status:** Imagine having a 'daily diary' bot on your intranet site. At anytime, people add their ideas, challenges, sentiment and more. Then automatically, that data gets analyzed in real time and creates your risk ledger and status reports.
- **Ask the Project Bot:** I mentioned this in the last section. We know there is far too much documentation, which is usually out of date, for people to make sense of. You can feed your bot your project documentation and let people ask it questions. When things change, you simply train your bot

on different data. As an example, let's assume you've fed it your project schedule with key dates. When the dates change, simply tell your bot: "when people ask when UAT is, tell them it's now July 1 instead of June 1. Tell them we changed the date because the customer wasn't ready and they should contact biff@project.com for more details."

- **Status Reports and Summaries:** Another obvious one. Feed it your status reports and ask it to generate a response that shows what has changed since the last status report. To go even further, if you're using the idea from the first point here (Real-time status), ask it to summarize the sentiment of how the project is going and break it down by department, team, or role. Similar to the tips in the communications section, you can ask it to summarize information for stakeholders, customers, or any other role.

- **Talking Head Videos:** I worked somewhere where the change team did a 'news program' show for communicating updates. You could use a tool like D-ID [2] to create them automatically. You could also use the same tool for just about any talking head video content and you can train it with your voice, or even clone yourself so it looks like it really is you!

Let your imagination run wild, and remember, you can talk to AI like a human. If you are having a problem figuring out how it can make your life easier, especially when you're assigned to 7 projects, ask it:

> *I am overwhelmed. I am going to dump a bunch of project charters, status reports, emails and more and want you to create a project summary and up-to-date status of each of the 7 projects. The name of the files follow this pattern: project name - artefact type.pdf.*

It may ask you some followup questions, but you can also ask it if it needs more information before it can help.

5. Better Meetings

Many meeting tools have, or are in progress, of adding AI capability. Creating 'minutes' is a drag, and a huge time-suck. Here's how you can use AI to make your meetings more effective.

- **Realtime Translation:** Zoom has this built in, it can generate subtitles in multiple languages automatically. Tools like Noty.ai can do the same, but also generate searchable transcripts and create summaries of the meeting.
- **Continuous Improvement:** At the end of the meeting, ask people to toss a comment in the MS Teams, or Zoom chat. If you're lucky enough to be doing this in-person, use sticky notes. Feed that into AI like this: "I am uploading meeting minutes from Jan 1. The topic was <whatever> and <these roles> were present. I'm going to upload their feedback about how effective it was. Analyze it and give me suggestions for making it better next time." After the next meeting, open up the same thread and feed it the next meeting details. Remember AI stays in context, so it'll remember the details about all the meetings you add.
- **Prep, Agenda Writing etc:** This one is also obvious. Ask AI: "I'm scheduling a meeting for <roles> about <topic>, write me an agenda, an email invite, a 'how to prepare' email, and a reminder email. The possibilities here are endless, it's like having an admin assistant. This would be more difficult, but you could integrate your calendar and meeting booking room service to do that automatically too.
- **Transcription, Translation and more:** Vimeo has this built it, and you can protect your content so it's only accessible from within your company's firewall. It will generate transcripts automatically and you can ask AI to generate a summary of the meeting, key points, who was there and more. You can also translate them, or create sub-titles automatically. As mentioned, Vimeo does this and I imagine

there are plenty of other tools that can as well. Also as mentioned, Noty.ai can do this in real-time with Zoom and Google Meet. I assume Co-Pilot has something for those of you using MS Teams.

6. Content Creation

This is another area where AI shines. Again, content creation is an aspect of all of the six points in this chapter so for this section, I'll add some extra bits I didn't cover in the other five sections.

From text, to images, to video, you can literally create anything, instantly. The inspiration for this book was actually a blog post that I didn't end up posting. I started writing it 'old school' and I was using a few prompts and responses from GPT-4 and then it hit me. This post is going to be 400 pages, why not put it in a book instead?

If I had to guess, I wrote 70% of this, AI wrote the other 30%. AI could have written it all and I could have trained it on my style by using my other books, but I love writing and actually want to do most of it myself. With the help of AI, I wrote this entire book in 3 days from start to finish.

Here's how I got started, along with ideas and possibilities for content creation.

- I wrote the structure, 3 Practical Ways to use AI in Change Management. I created the bullet points, gathered the data from surveys, screenshots etc and used these prompts:
- Write me a blog post based on <this content>.
- Include your ideas about how AI will change change management.
- ask me what other information you'd need to do this
- create 5 variations of this title: "3 Practical Ways to use AI in Change Management.

- create 20 social media posts for LinkedIn, target audience is \<these people\>.
- create 3 featured images for the blog post (Note, after I did that, GPT-4 said I had to do that one at a time).

Some will say AI generated content is obvious and robotic sounding. I agree, but you can tell it to change the tone and train it to sound like you. Plus, it's always a good idea that you read what it generates and tweak it. Here's what else it can do:

- **Non-Technical overviews:** Feed it the documents from the 3rd party system you're implementing and ask it to create highlights of the most important features that describe how it affects leaders, or end users. This is insanely powerful. Think of all the implementation docs, technical manuals, vendor notes/patches etc. Sometimes you, or maybe the project manager, are tasked with reading those and sending out communications. AI can do this instantly for you.
- **What's Changing Snippets:** When I make product updates for the startup I'm working for, I feed AI my list of user stories and acceptance criteria and it generates my release notes for me. Think of how powerful this can be for cutting change records, especially if you're in a regulated environment.
- **Images and Infographics:** Images are tricky. GPT-4 uses Dall-E which is also used by Mid Journey. Mid Journey is basically a Discord server where you add a prompt to make an image. I've found this to be the most flakey of all AI tools. Flakey because you have be very good at prompts and describing what you want. Sometimes the images generated by Dall-E via GPT-4 are not even close to what I see in my brain.

As an example, I asked GPT-4 to write a 3 paragraph summary about the difference between project management and change management. I didn't actually use that content in this book because I didn't like it. Then I asked it to create an infographic that shows the differences, here's what it created:

Ouch!

So yes, there's a little more effort and learning curve for creating images!

Is Your Job Safe?

If AI can do all of this, is your job safe? Yes, of course it is. I'd highly recommend you get out in front of AI. Much like how I was forced into multi-skilling my self from a simple web designer to someone who could program, run servers, design graphics, and do front-end and back-end work, you're always going to be asked to do more with less.

The more you can leverage AI, the less stress you'll have, the more efficient you'll be and the less likely you're organization is going to need to hire and over-specialize their change related roles.

Consider the holy trinity of a change team: the change manger, project manager and comms person. All of that work can absolutely, positively be done by one person with AI, depending on context of course.

Now imagine all three of these people throw their titles out the window and start using and sharing how to use AI in change projects. That team of three will absolutely kick ass.

CHAPTER 8
WHY AI? WHY NOW?

T'm going to speed through this chapter because as a change manager you already know the importance of unpacking the 'why' of the change.

I recommend you use a change canvas! [1]

AI moves incredibly fast. Here's all the proof I need to back that statement up. I finished writing this book on Friday, January 12, 2024. Today is January 17, and I'm revising the final copy thanks to help from my friend and trusty copy-editor Julia.[2]

In less than 5 days, this is what's changed in the AI landscape:

- Open CEO Sam Altman announced GPT-5 and said right now, "AI is the stupidest it will ever be".
- Microsoft opened up access to GPT-4 through their Co-Pilot platform.
- Microsoft also made Co-Pilot available to all Office 365 users and launched Co-Pilot Pro.
- Channel One News will launch as the 'worlds first' generative AI news channel.[3]

- Amazon launched an AI tool that will answer shopper's questions.

And that is only a few cherry-picked examples.

The best AI strategy you can employ now is to start trying it in order to figure out what it's capable of.

Then you can worry about shoehorning it into your strategy. Reason being, a *wait-and-see strategy* simply will not work. By the time you've created a *good enough* strategy, it'll be useless because the landscape will have significantly shifted.

You will not be able to sufficiently plan your way through an AI project. Get in a room, open this book and start using the prompts. After an hour, your AI strategy should be reasonably clear. If that's not enough information, try these prompts:

> *I am in <industry whatever>. Our organization <does these things>. We are conservative and skeptical of AI. How can AI help us?*
>
> *What do you think the consequences will be if our organization waits to adopt AI?*
>
> *Give how AI has evolved until now, can you predict what it will be capable of in a year? 2 years? 5 years?*

This chapter might be making the *planners* uncomfortable and I agree. I wrote it because most companies suffer from *corporate me-too-ism*. Meaning, they see a bunch of stuff all over LinkedIn and want to do it too for the fear of being left out. This is the case with agile, which sometimes is referred to as 'new ways of working' because people got sick of the word agile.

Some call this agile-in-name-only, or an exercise in change theatre, meaning, the change was initiated for the fear of the possible consequence of *not* doing it, not because it was the right change.

A client approached me and wanted to implement change agility[4] in their organization. That was the term they wanted to use, not Lean Change Management.

I poked, and poked, and poked, and no one could ever answer why they wanted to do it. They were, and still are, one of the world biggest and most profitable organizations. The people are incredibly competent, driven and curious. I remember telling them that they could have a 47,000 step-based approach to change and everything they touched would still turn into gold.

Long-story short, we sprinkled a bit of change agility dust around and they thinned out some of their change processes, but it wasn't any earth-shattering transformation of how they did change.

To me, this was an exercise in corporate me-too-ism. That is, they had heard and read so much stuff about Lean Change, they wanted to do it too.

The same thing will happen with AI.

Someone will post an AI case study and the world will go ga-ga over it. Leaders will demand an AI strategy without providing much direction. Unscrupulous vendors will start promoting certifications and other nonsense for using AI, and the gold rush will be on.

> Pro Tip: I 100% guarantee someone in your organization is going to get duped by a tool vendor selling you promises that their software will ensure successful change using AI. Do not fall for it. You'll see exactly how to use AI for predictive analysis starting in Chapter 12.

You can use the ideas in this book to help leaders understand what AI is, and how they might want to use it.

CHAPTER 9

THE ETHICAL
CONSIDERATIONS OF AI

Ethics. Good ol' ethics.

This is going to be a huge challenge with AI. Remember, AI is only as good as the data it's trained on, the algorithms it uses, and the instructions and prompts you give it.

If you remember from Chapter 4, Microsoft's Co-Pilot was suggesting its own products in response to analyzing data whereas GPT-4 was not. Is that ethical on Microsoft's behalf?

Meh, I guess so. It's not a surprise. It is clearly agenda-laden, but is that really a big deal?

Another example: In 2022 before Custom GPTs existed, I used a GitHub project to create an 'ask my book' bot. I could never really get it to work right so I put it on the shelf. In 2023, I built a Custom GPT and trained it on all three of my books, *Change Agility*, *Lean Change Management* and *The Art and Science of Change*.

I told the bot to disclose how it had been trained, the data that was included and what it was designed to do. I mentioned ADKAR in Lean Change Management so when I was testing the bot, I asked it to explain what Lean Change Management was and it gave me an answer that included some information about ADKAR.

Here's where the ethics come into play. Should I tell the bot to exclude any 'competing framework' information? For the record, I don't consider any of Prosci's stuff to be a competitor to Lean Change. It's like saying an Audi e-Tron RS (Lean Change) is a competitor to a 1981 Toyota Corolla (Prosci). Sure, both are cars, but one of them is infinitely cooler, and clearly better than the other!

> Spoiler alert, I did not give my bot that instruction because that wouldn't be ethical in my view. I wrote it because I thought it would be funny.

I don't imagine AI ethics will be a big topic until 2025 or later. It's going to take that long for enough people to start using it before everyone starts complaining about bias and manipulation. But make no mistake, society will want checks and balances in place, so we are going to have to rely on Big Tech to police themselves.

In mid-2003, Geoffrey Hinton, who was an AI pioneer at Google, resigned so he could speak about the risks and ethics of AI freely without fear of persecution - or prosecution, or both? - from Google. I whole-heartedly believe most people are good, but I do not believe for one second the 'ethical guidelines' published by Big Tech companies are based in any sort of reality. Their goal is making money, period.

When I use AI, I follow my own ethical guidelines:

- I will not train this bot to push my agenda.
- I will always train my bot to disclose its intention, the instructions used to create it and the data it was trained on.
- I will update the bot if any user or customer finds something that looks like plagiarism or agenda-pushing.

At Lean Change, my bots are designed to help people understand Lean Change and give them ideas to modernize their approach to change.

At the startup I work for, my bots are designed to aid employment specialists help their autistic clients find and keep jobs.

It'll be up to you to figure out how to sort out the ethical mess AI will cause in your organization[1].

- How transparent should our bot be about this change?
- We know corporate comms are full of BS, should our AI sugar coat things and keep the brutal truth hidden?
- Who can we trust to train the AI and feed it data?
- How open should our AI be? Restrict it to our data, our training, or let it evolve and learn on its own?
- What about copyright material? Should we use it and cite it, hope we get away with it, or ask first? (For the record, Open AI Sam Altman said it would be impossible to create content via AI with using copyright material.[2]

These are just a few considerations, so I'll end this chapter with what AI thinks the ethical problems will be.

What ethical conundrums will organizations face when creating their AI strategy?

GPT-4's Response

~

Companies implementing an AI strategy face several ethical conundrums that need careful consideration and management. These ethical challenges include:

1. Bias and Fairness: AI systems are only as unbiased as the data they're trained on. If the training data contains biases, the AI's decisions and recommendations can perpetuate and amplify these biases, leading to unfair outcomes. This is particularly critical in areas like hiring, lending, and law enforcement.

2. Privacy: AI often requires large amounts of data, which can include sensitive personal information. Ensuring the privacy and security of this data is a major ethical concern, especially with regulations like GDPR and CCPA mandating strict data privacy practices.

3. Transparency and Explainability: Many AI models, especially deep learning systems, are often seen as "black boxes" due to their complexity. Companies face the challenge of making AI decisions transparent and understandable, both for regulatory compliance and to maintain public trust.

4. Job Displacement: The automation capabilities of AI can lead to job displacement, raising ethical questions about the responsibility of companies to their employees. This includes managing the transition for workers whose jobs are automated and retraining them for new roles.

5. Dependence on Technology: Over-reliance on AI can lead to a loss of critical human skills and judgment. Companies must consider how to balance AI use with human

oversight, especially in critical decision-making processes.

6. Security: AI systems can be targeted by malicious actors, leading to security breaches. Ethical use of AI involves ensuring robust security measures to prevent misuse of AI systems.

7. Global Inequality: As AI technology advances, there's a risk of widening the gap between companies, and countries, with access to cutting-edge AI and those without. This raises concerns about global inequalities being exacerbated by unequal access to AI technology.

8. Environmental Impact: Training large AI models can be energy-intensive, raising concerns about the environmental impact of AI, especially regarding carbon footprint and sustainability.

9. Accountability: Determining accountability for decisions made by AI systems is challenging. Companies must consider who is responsible when an AI system causes harm or makes an error — the AI developers, the users, or the AI itself?

10. Consumer Manipulation: AI's ability to analyze and predict human behavior can be used in ways that manipulate consumers, such as in targeted advertising. Companies face ethical considerations about the extent to which they use AI to influence consumer behavior.

Addressing these ethical conundrums requires a thoughtful approach, including establishing clear ethical guidelines, investing in bias detection and correction, ensuring transparency and security, and engaging in open dialogue with stakeholders.

~

Some of that sounds pretty scary. Think about being on an AI strategic implementation and having to worry about all of those things. You'll never get started.

To close this chapter, I rely on my gut. If I feel icky, I've done something wrong.

CHAPTER 10
USING CUSTOM GPTS

For this, and the remaining chapters, I will be using Open AI's GPT-4. As a reminder, GPT-4 is current as of April 2023 and is only available to GPT Plus subscribers for $20 a month. That might have changed so head over to chat.openai.com.

GPT-3.5 is free to use, but is limited to data from January 2022. As full disclosure, most of the content from here on out is AI generated. I'll list all the prompts I use and add commentary and stories to support what GPT-4 creates for me.

Everything I've mentioned in Chapter 5 (Change Management After AI) is possible to do manually with GPT-4 or via a Custom GPT.

What is a Custom GPT?

A Custom GPT is bot you can create at chat.openai.com to do whatever you want. As an example, I created 'Ask Lean Change', which is a bot that will allow you to ask my books questions.

You must be a GPT-Plus subscriber to do this. Here's a longer description generated by GPT-4.

A custom GPT (Generative Pre-trained Transformer) refers to a version of the GPT model that has been tailored or fine-tuned for specific applications or to meet the unique needs of a particular user or organization. Unlike standard GPT models like GPT-3 or GPT-4, which are general-purpose and designed to handle a wide range of tasks, a custom GPT is adapted to perform optimally in a more focused domain or set of tasks. Here are some key aspects of custom GPTs:

1. Specialized Training Data: Custom GPT models are often trained or fine-tuned on a specific dataset relevant to the desired application. For example, a custom GPT for legal applications might be trained on a large corpus of legal documents and case law.

2. Tailored Outputs: The model is adapted to generate outputs that are more aligned with the specific language, tone, style, or technical content required by the user. This can enhance the model's effectiveness in niche applications.

3. Improved Accuracy in Specific Domains: By focusing on a particular domain, custom GPTs can offer more accurate and relevant responses within that domain, as they are more attuned to its specific nuances and vocabulary.

4. Adaptation to User Preferences: Custom GPTs can also be adjusted to align with the user's preferences, such as a certain writing style, format, or even incorporating specific branding elements in generated content.

5. Enhanced Privacy and Security: For organizations concerned about data privacy, custom GPTs can be trained on internal datasets, ensuring that the model operates within a controlled environment and adheres to organizational data policies.

6. Integration with Specific Systems: Custom GPTs can be integrated into specific systems or workflows, providing seamless interaction with existing technological infrastructure.

7. Use Case Examples: Examples include custom GPTs for creating technical manuals, generating specific types of marketing content, automating customer service responses in a particular industry, or

assisting with medical diagnosis based on medical literature.

Developing a custom GPT requires expertise in machine learning and natural language processing, as well as access to appropriate training data. Organizations may collaborate with AI developers or use platforms provided by companies like OpenAI, which offer the ability to fine-tune models based on specific requirements.

How to Create a Custom GPT

At chat.openai.com, click 'explore' then 'create'. The configuration screen will be displayed, but it might look a bit different than this:

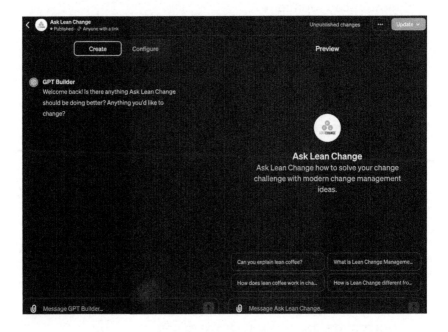

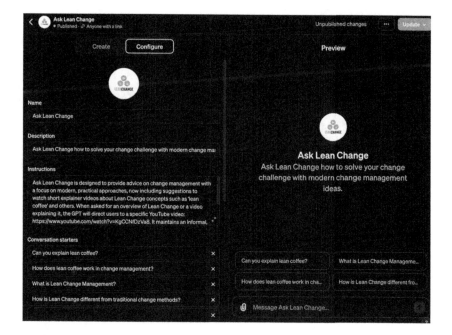

These are the main things you'll need to do:

1. **Name**: What do you want to call it?
2. **Description**: What is displayed on the public 'explore' page.
3. Instructions: What this is, what is does and how it should behave.
4. **Conversation Starters**: Suggested prompts you want users to use
5. **Knowledge**: Here's where it gets fun. You can upload whatever data you want, or connect it to any source like Airtable, Google Docs, or any API. As an example, 'Ask Lean Change' is trained on my books and my Youtube channel content.

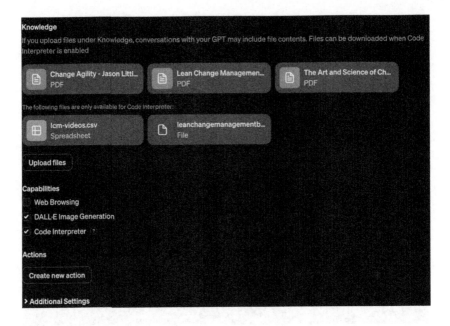

Note that under Capabilities, I have disabled web browsing. This means it'll always use only the data I upload. Again, consider the ethics of doing this. If you disable web browsing, your Custom GPT will only use the data you give it. Imagine you're making a Change Management Knowledge-base bot. Now you upload your own proprietary information, and train it on giving responses that will lead to more business. Is that ethical if you name the bot, "Change Management Co-Pilot"?

I configured it this way because the intention of the bot is to "ask my book a question", I don't want internet searches cluttering up the responses.

- **Dall-E Image Generation**: When enabled, users can create images from your knowledge base.
- **Code Interpreter**: This must be enabled to do analysis of your data.

Using Actions

Since this is a non-technical book, I am not going to confuse you with too many details. You will need to be familiar with how APIs work.

That said, this solves the problem of having to re-upload data. Remember how many times I mentioned real-time data analysis in this book? You would need to create actions that allow your bot to access that data, or use automation tools like Zapier, or Make to feed it.

I will say, if you are mildly technical and understand how APIs work, you can ask your bot to create the necessary details to create your actions.

> *I want to use data from a Google spreadsheet to power the data in this bot, how can I do that?*

GPT-4 will give you some generic instructions.

Based on how GPT-4 responds, you might follow up with:

> *I will upload a CSV file of my Google doc. Use it to create a schema and include all the details necessary to create an action that will grab data from <the url of your google sheet>*

That's as far as I'll take the actions section, I'll admit it was a little tricky getting the *State of Change Management* Airtable[1] data to be read and used, but once it was done, it was done and now I don't have to do anything.

Publishing Your Bot

There are three settings for publishing your bot:

- **Only me:** Only you can see and use it.

- **Anyone with a link:** Anyone who has the link.
- **Anyone:** Public, and listed in the Custom GPT store under the 'explore' section.

Using Your Bot

A giant caveat for using this bot is users must be on a GPT Plus plan. If you want to use a Custom GPT internally, you would need to use a service like BotPress[2] to do that. There are hundreds of bot embedding tools out there but at the time of writing this book, Open AI has not provided a way to do that.

The other option is using Open AI's Assistant tool which requires some technical knowledge.

Training Your Bot

On the Create tab (see screenshot earlier in this chapter), you'll have a split window. On the left is where you'll train your bot. On the right is responses your bot will generate. Here are prompts you can use to train you bot:

when people ask who created this bot tell them <whatever>

when people ask why this bot exists, tell them <whatever>

what format do you expect the data to be in that I want to train you on?

what prompts can I ask you to customize my bot?

when people ask about <this topic> ask them if they want to see a short video tutorial. If they say yes, send them to this YouTube video <insert link>

I want the tone of your responses to be playful and informal

There are thousands of questions you can ask, but a good way to train your bot is to start asking it questions you think your users will ask.

In the Preview window, start asking it questions. Once you see the responses, you can update the instructions to make the response better. Your bot will learn and evolve, but it takes time and patience to train it to be as useful as it can be.

Also, you can ask you bot what it can do. For my 'Ask Lean Change' bot, I wasn't sure if it could email me if someone asked it to do that. I asked:

> *are you able to send me an email? for example, if someone asked a question about how they could contact the author, could you ask them to create a message, add their email address and then send me an email?*

It replied with:

∼

```
I've updated Ask Lean Change to clarify that it
cannot send emails or facilitate direct contact
with    individuals.    If    someone    asks    about
contacting  the  author  or  similar  requests,  the
GPT  will  suggest  visiting  the  official  website  or
social  media  profiles  for  contact  information.

Is  there  anything  else  you  would  like  to  adjust
or  add?
```

∼

Then I added:

ok, if someone asks to get in contact, direct them to lean-change.org/contact

To which it replied:

~

```
I've updated the behavior to guide users to
leanchange.org/contact for contact information
when they inquire about how to get in touch with
the author or related queries, while making it
clear that the GPT cannot send emails or directly
facilitate contact.

Is there anything else you would like to update
or modify?
```

~

Again, remember that you can talk to your bot like a person, and it stays in context. If you're ever unsure of how to train it, ask it!

Tips for Creating Your Bot by GTP-4

I asked GPT-4 to give me tips for training my Custom GPT and this is what it replied with:

~

```
Creating a custom GPT (Generative Pre-trained
Transformer) involves several steps, primarily
focused on fine-tuning a pre-existing GPT model
with specific data and parameters to suit your
unique requirements. Here's a simplified overview
of the process:
```

Define Your Objective:

- Clearly define what you want your custom
  GPT to do. This includes understanding the
  specific domain, style, or type of tasks
  you want the model to perform.

Gather and Prepare Your Training Data:

- Collect a dataset that is representative of
  the tasks you want your custom GPT to
  perform. This data should be relevant to
  your domain and include examples of the
  type of output you expect from the model.
- Clean and preprocess the data to make it
  suitable for training. This might involve
  removing irrelevant information, correcting
  errors, and formatting the data
  consistently.

Choose a Base GPT Model:

- Select a base GPT model to fine-tune. This
  could be a publicly available model like
  GPT-3 or GPT-4, depending on your
  requirements and access to these models.

Fine-Tuning the Model:

- Fine-tuning involves training the base GPT
  model on your specific dataset. This
  process adjusts the model's weights and
  parameters to better align with your data,
  enhancing its performance on your desired
  tasks.

- Use machine learning platforms or tools that support model training. For GPT models, this might involve using APIs or platforms provided by OpenAI or other AI service providers.

Test and Evaluate the Model:

- After fine-tuning, evaluate the model's performance to ensure it meets your expectations. Test it with real-world examples and scenarios to check its accuracy and relevance.
- Collect feedback and iteratively improve the model by adjusting training data or fine-tuning parameters as needed.

Deployment and Integration:

- Once satisfied with the model's performance, deploy it into your application or workflow.
- Ensure that the model is integrated seamlessly with your existing systems and that there are interfaces for users to interact with it.

Ongoing Monitoring and Maintenance:

- Continuously monitor the model's performance to ensure it remains accurate and effective over time.
- Regularly update the model with new data to keep it relevant and improve its capabilities.

Ethical Considerations and Compliance:

- Address any ethical considerations, especially around data privacy and bias.
- Ensure your use of AI complies with relevant regulations and ethical guidelines.

Creating a custom GPT model requires expertise in machine learning, natural language processing, and data science. If you don't have this exper- tise in-house, consider partnering with AI devel- opment firms or consulting experts in the field. Additionally, be aware of the costs and resources involved, as training and maintaining custom AI models can be resource-intensive.

If you're not that technical, using a Custom GPT or even just the GPT-4 interface can say you tons of time.

Finally, if you've been forbidden from using AI, you can configure your Custom GPT to be used only by you and you won't have to worry about your data being available to the general public.

CHAPTER 11
USING NO CODE AND APIS

Again, since this is not a technical book, I am going to limit this chapter to pointing you towards possibilities.

No- and Low- Code tools help non-technical people build stuff. Whether it's websites, mobile apps, or simple applications, once you discover and start using these tools, you'll be much less reliant on IT and developers for things.

Yes, there is a giant caveat there. What about security? Who maintains it? What if management finds out?

Google spreadsheets and Excel are the two most used BI and application tools used by business people. Every organization has running jokes about being 'run on spreadsheets'. They're simple to use and don't require IT or developers.

Think of No- and Low- Code tools as Google Sheets and Excel on steroids.

Here are a few tools you might want to look at.

Airtable

Airtable[1] is vastly superior to Google Sheets. It's basically an online database that looks like Google Sheets. There are plenty of plugins and templates that will let you do just about anything from analysis to reports/charts and more. There are also plenty of AI related plugins and you can use the data as a source for your Custom GPT actions.

Zapier

Zapier[2] is an automation tool, not an AI tool. Essentially is allows you to connect any system without needing to write code. As an example, you can have Zapier email you when someone adds a line of data to your Airtable, or Google Sheet. If you're using Slack, you could also have it ping a channel in Slack, or a user, or any combination of public or private channel or users. Zapier has thousands of recipes to start with. It does mislead users a little by referring to itself as AI, but it's not. You have to connect your systems together and tell it exactly what to do.

Make.com

Make.com[3] used to be called Integromat and it is essentially Zapier on steroids. Non-technical users can use it, but it's more targeted at technical people. Not developers, just technical people. It has built in storage, thousands of recipes and it connects with just about anything. The interface is much better as well. It's similar to designing a logic-based flow chart so it's easier to visualize the flow of your automation than Zapier is.

Bubble.io

Bubble.io[4] is an application building tool. It is big. It is overwhelming for non-technical people, but it is incredibly powerful. There are plenty of AI plugins that would allow you to do everything I mention in this book. The best part, you can secure it and also integrate it into whatever SSO (single sign-on) service your organization uses.

There are tens of thousands of No- and Low- Code tools, I only mentioned the ones I think are the easiest to use for non-technical folks. I also have a *Build Stuff with No Code* YouTube channel[5] specifically for non-technical people who want to get started.

Enterprise AI and Security

Up until now, all the tools and ideas I've mentioned can be used by anyone, but your corporate IT department will not like it. There is a huge risk in putting internal information in a SaaS solution without IT's involvement.

The most secure, and slowest, way to implementing AI is through an API.

GPT-4 explains it like this:

∾

An API, or Application Programming Interface, is like a messenger or an intermediary that allows different software applications to communicate with each other. Imagine you're in a restaurant: you have a menu of choices (the software application), a waiter who takes your order (the API), and the kitchen where your food is prepared (the server). Just like the waiter who communicates your order to the kitchen and then brings your food back to you, an API takes your requests (like clicking a button on an app), tells the system what you want, and then returns the system's response back to you. This process enables the apps and services you use to share data and perform tasks together smoothly, almost like a fluent conversation between different software languages.

~

To do this, you must have *some* developer skills. If you're mildly technical you could convert your Custom GPT to use the Assistants API and then create the frontend with Bubble.

As mentioned, this isn't a technical book, but I'm sure some of you would be intrigued enough to start tinkering! I will again take the lazy way out, and ask GPT-4 to describe the Assistants API in a non-technical way:

~

OpenAI's Assistants API, in a non-technical sense, can be thought of as a highly advanced digital assistant, much more sophisticated than the standard assistants you might find in smartphones or smart home devices. Imagine having a personal assistant who not only understands and responds to your spoken or typed requests but can also write, summarize information, answer complex questions, and even generate creative content based on your instructions.

This assistant, powered by OpenAI's cutting-edge AI technology, can understand and process natural language — meaning it can interpret and respond to the way humans naturally speak or write. You can ask it to do a variety of tasks, like drafting emails, creating content, summarizing lengthy documents, or even generating coding

```
scripts, and it does so in a conversational
manner.
```

```
What makes OpenAI's Assistants API remarkable is
its ability to learn from a vast amount of infor-
mation and its adaptability to different tasks.
It's like having a super-intelligent, multi-
skilled assistant who is always learning and
improving its ability to help you. This tech-
nology is accessible through an interface (API)
that allows businesses and developers to inte-
grate this smart assistant into their own soft-
ware applications, websites, or digital products,
enhancing the capabilities and user experience of
their offerings.
```

Interacting with AI through an API will always be more secure. Your context matters. I've worked in some organizations that used hosted product requirements software for managing software projects. For security reasons, we were allowed to store anything that had internal IP, customer info, or other sensitive information.

While security is obviously important, you can still dabble in AI, just use fake data so you can at least prove the benefits to your stakeholders.

Then you can wait 9 years for IT to implement it.

CHAPTER 12

IDEAS, POSSIBILITIES AND EXAMPLES

I n Chapter 5, I teased out six things with ideas and possibilities for using AI in change management. This and all following chapters will go into details with examples of what I've done and prompts you might want to try out.

Here are some notes that'll help you navigate the following chapters:

- I made the ideas as simple and accessible as possible. That means even if you are the least technical person on the planet, you can copy and paste these prompts into GTP-4 with no barrier.
- Oh, I am using GPT-4 for all the examples. I'll also mention some supporting tools along the way. If you want to use GPT-4, you'll need a GPT Plus subscription otherwise you can use GPT 3.5 for free. The responses will be a bit different between the two.
- It is possible to automate everything I will mention in the following chapters, but you'll need some technical skill to do that.

- I will mention often that there is some manual work copy/pasting data into spreadsheets or Airtable. If you're technical, you'll cringe, but if you're not, odds are you're already duct-taping things together with Excel or Google Sheets, so this is basically the same thing.
- There will be some overlap between examples from chapter to chapter, and some of the ideas will be similar so you can likely use prompts I suggested in the 'designing training sessions' section for 'content creation' or other areas.
- You can always to go https://leanchange.org/ai for more up to date content.

CHAPTER 13

DESIGNING TRAINING SESSIONS

I always do custom training sessions. I never, or rarely, run pre-packaged training because most of the changes I work on are transformational in nature. That means agile adoption or transformation, or installing new ways of working, or doing tune-ups and more.

I'll be more specific with this example. A client hired me to help with an 'agile practices tune up'. They wanted me to do a couple of retrospectives to help them figure out what to change, and then do some agile and scrum training. Actually, today was the day I finished the training so this example is nice and fresh!

I used Miro for the session as it was a hybrid meeting. After everyone added their questions, I took a screenshot and ask prompted GPT-4 like this:

I am running a training session about agile techniques, in particular scrum. Can you analyze the sticky notes in the picture I am uploading and generate a summary of the questions people are asking? I'd also like to know what topics are mentioned the most, and if you can, find what their most common pain points are.

I'm not going to post the whole response as it's quite long, but here was the summary:

～

```
Based  on  these  points,  the  training  should
address  role  definitions  within  scrum  teams,
strategies  for  handling  changes  and  unexpected
issues  within  a  sprint,  effective  communication
methods,  workload  management,  and  best  practices
for  incorporating  technical  debt  and  refactoring.
It's  also  clear  that  there's  an  interest  in  prac-
tical,  actionable  advice  on  applying  agile  prin-
ciples  day-to-day.
```

～

I did this in real-time and yes, I could have affinity mapped these and gleaned similar insights, but this took 15 seconds to do with GPT-4 and my brain didn't have to do anything.

Here's another example. Suppose you are planning a training session in advance, you can do all sorts of cool things. As I mentioned, I always do customized training so I am in the habit of sending surveys, or emails to get some insights about what people want to get out of it.

Here was my prompt:

> *I am organizing a training session and I asked people to tell me what they hope to get out of it. Can you analyze the responses and tell me if there are common things people want to learn?*

GPT-4 responded with an eight bullet point summary, followed by the 4 main topics that I should focus on.

~

The responses you've received from your associates regarding the upcoming training session reveal several common themes and expectations:

1. Adoption of Agile/Lean Methods: There's a recurring interest in learning about agile and lean methodologies. People are looking to understand how these can be implemented to improve workflows and processes.
2. Improvement in Processes and Systems: Many responses indicate a desire to improve existing systems and processes that may be outdated or inefficient. This includes a willingness to change and adapt to new strategies.
3. Enhancement of Work Environment: Some associates are eager to create a happier and more productive work environment. This ties in with the desire to improve collaboration and job satisfaction.
4. Effective Response to Change: There's an acknowledgment that the business environment has changed, and with it, a need for processes to evolve to remain relevant and effective.
5. Desire for Efficiency and Enjoyment in Work: A few responses highlight the aim to find a balance between efficient work and enjoying the process, with an outcome of producing great work.
6. Expectation Management: There is a mix of anticipation and skepticism. While many are

looking forward to the training, at least one individual is unsure about the relevance of the session.

7. Seeking Practical Outcomes: Participants are hoping to see practical, tangible results from the training, such as faster delivery times for tasks and projects, and real-world applications that will benefit their roles.

8. Mindset Shift: There's an underlying theme of wanting to shift to a more flexible, responsive mindset that aligns with contemporary business practices.

From these points, it seems that the training session should focus on:

- Introducing agile and lean principles.
- Demonstrating how these methodologies can improve current working systems.
- Showcasing the tangible benefits of adopting these approaches.
- Addressing the changes in the business environment and how agile/lean can help navigate these changes.
- Ensuring the training is interactive and demonstrates practical applications to engage skeptical participants.

When planning your session, consider these shared interests and concerns to ensure the training is relevant and valuable to your associates

~

Then I asked it a follow-up:

does it sound like people are excited about it? what's the general sentiment?

~

The general sentiment toward the training session appears to be mostly positive, with several individuals expressing excitement and a strong desire to learn and improve existing processes through agile and lean methodologies. Many are looking forward to the session, indicating a proactive approach to personal and professional development and an understanding of the need for adaptation in response to business changes.

However, the sentiment is not universally positive. At least one response suggests skepticism or a lack of understanding of the purpose of the training, indicating a perception that it might be a waste of time. Another flat-out refusal with "No thanks" shows resistance to the idea.

In summary, while the predominant sentiment is one of anticipation and optimism about learning new ways to improve work processes, there is a mix of emotions, and a small fraction of the responses reflect hesitation or resistance. It's important to acknowledge and address these varied sentiments during the session to ensure that it is inclusive and addresses the concerns of all participants.

~

And finally, I asked it:

for the question I asked about creating the training session, could you suggest some good interactive exercises I can do at the beginning of the session to grab people's attention?

and it replied with:

~

To engage participants right from the start of your agile techniques and scrum training session, you can use interactive exercises that are both informative and energizing. Here are some suggestions:

- Agile Ball Point Game: This is a popular game to introduce people to the principles of Agile and the importance of iteration. The goal is to pass a ball around a circle of people as quickly and accurately as possible. After each round, participants discuss how to improve the process, demonstrating the agile principles of inspecting and adapting.
- Scrum Simulation with Legos: Use Legos to simulate a scrum sprint. Participants form small teams and are given a set of requirements to build a specific structure within a timebox. After the sprint, hold a retrospective to discuss what went well, what didn't, and how to improve the next sprint.
- Product Box: Provide materials for participants to design a box for a product

that would be sold using agile methodology. This helps people understand the importance of vision and clear communication of features and benefits. It also introduces the concept of the Minimum Viable Product (MVP).

- User Story Mapping: Have participants write down features of a hypothetical product on sticky notes. Then, as a group, they can arrange these notes on a wall or table to create a user story map, which helps them visualize the product backlog and understand how user stories fit into the bigger picture.

- Priority Poker: Similar to planning poker but for prioritizing features or user stories. Each participant gets to 'bet' on the features they believe should be top priority, fostering discussion and collaboration on what is most important in the product backlog.

- Scrum Roles Play: Assign participants to different scrum roles (Product Owner, Scrum Master, Team Member) and give them a scenario to act out. This can highlight the responsibilities and dynamics of each role within the scrum framework.

- Impromptu Networking: A quick-paced activity where participants share their experiences with agile and scrum within a very short timeframe (like 2 minutes) with as many other participants as possible. This not only serves as an icebreaker but also helps to surface common experiences and challenges.

- The Sailboat Retrospective: An exercise that can be used at the beginning to set the stage. Participants draw a boat, rocks, clouds, and a sun. They then write down what they feel will propel the team forward (wind), what will be a challenge (rocks), what they hope to achieve (sun), and any concerns (clouds).

These exercises can help illustrate agile principles and scrum practices in an engaging way, encouraging participation and setting a collaborative tone for the rest of the training session.

~

I am going to stop there, but here are some suggestions for prompts you could follow up with:

The ball point game sounds cool, tell me how to do it and if possible, give me a URL that has instructions

I like the idea of networking, but this team all knows each other. What would be some good questions I could use that would shake things up a little?

can you tell me specifically what agile value and principles, or principles would be learned from the ball point game?

I have decided on the ball point game. Can you write me 3 emails. 1) an exciting one to the participants that will tease the game enough to get people interested without giving it all away? 2) to the leadership team that describes the objective, general idea behind the game and what they'll get out of it? 3) a thank you to the participants that I'll send after I send them a survey. I'll come back to this thread and upload a picture of the feedback or paste in text

Oh, and can you create a slide presentation of instructions? (note I am still in context, so I don't have to tell GPT-4 anything else.

Now, you could make the argument the interaction I just had would be the same as using a search engine. The difference is that it only took 1 minute and my brain didn't have to do anything.

I barely scratched the surface of how creative prompts could do most, or all, of the work for me. Thinking back to doing this 'the old way', I might have:

- Had my own mini-brainstorm session.
- Posted something on a forum for ideas.
- Just used the same thing I did before and missed out on a better game.
- Try to remember where I put the PDFs of instructions.
- Maybe 30-45 minutes typing the emails.

Ideas for Prompts

We are starting an agile transformation. I'm new to agile. Can you write me a summary of what it is, targeted at executives?

Suggest 3 activities I could use to teach executives what agile is

I have a liftoff with stakeholders about a project that <what is this project for?>. I will upload the data showing what I've been asked to do. Can you suggest a good way to grab their attention at the beginning of the session?

Can you create an outline of this <upload your training manual>

My first training session didn't go well and I need to train another team. I am going to upload the feedback and the agenda along with the activities I did. Can you look for what I might have done wrong and suggest ideas for making the next one better?

I am creating a 'agile for change managers' training session. Can you brainstorm ideas that would be useful to go through? The attendees think Agile is all about software so I don't want to confuse them with 'agile mumbo-jumbo'

These prompts are conversation starters, if you look at my examples, that will give you clues in to follow prompts. Remember, AI stays in context so if it generates seven bullet points and they sound generic you can ask it:

can you expand on point 4?

I like point 3, can you generate instruction/slides/emails etc.

can you find any case studies about the activities used in point 2?

Finally, you know how to design training sessions. All you need to do is to create a few bullet points about what it is, who it's for, and learning objectives, and AI will do the rest.

CHAPTER 14

DATA ANALYSIS

A I shines at data analysis. Here are the prompts and details about how I use GPT-4 on the *State of Change Management* survey.

I collected the responses from Survey Monkey and downloaded a CSV file output. I simply pasted in the raw data without any formatting. I did this to test the bot before moving the data to Airtable so it's all automated.

> *I want help analyzing survey responses. I created a survey that was sent to change managers asking them what the most important lessons they learned in their careers was. Can you summarize the results and find 3 patterns in the data?*

GPT-4 Responded with:

∽

To assist you effectively with summarizing survey results and identifying patterns, I'll need some details about the survey data:

1. Survey Data: Can you provide the actual responses or a summary of the responses from the change managers? This could include key phrases, recurring themes, or direct quotes from the participants.
2. Number of Responses: How many individuals responded to the survey? This will help understand the sample size and diversity of insights.
3. Survey Questions: What specific questions were asked? Knowing the questions can help understand the context of the responses.
4. Additional Information: Any demographic or background information about the respondents that might be relevant (e.g., years of experience, industries represented).

With this information, I can help you analyze the responses, summarize the findings, and identify key patterns or lessons from the data.

~

I said:

The question was "what was the most important lesson you've learned about change management?. 74 people responded here are the raw responses: <copy and pasted the output from Survey Monkey>

GPT-4's Response:

~

Thank you for providing the survey data. Based on the raw responses from 74 change managers, here are three key patterns that emerge:

1. Importance of Leadership and Stakeholder Engagement: Many responses emphasized the critical role of senior management and stakeholder engagement. Phrases like "top management sponsorship is essential," "leadership plays a key role," and the need for a "single agreed shared purpose" suggest that successful change management depends heavily on active and committed leadership.

2. Cultural and Mindset Shifts: There is a strong pattern of recognizing that change management is not just about processes but also about people and their willingness to adopt new practices. Terms such as "culture and mindset trump everything else," "change is personal," and the importance of "employee engagement" indicate that addressing organizational culture and individual mindsets is paramount for effective change.

3. Adaptability and Flexibility: The third pattern indicates a move away from rigid, traditional methodologies toward a more adaptable and flexible approach. Responses such as "change is changing," "drop what isn't working," and the need to be

```
"flexible" and "adaptable to any type of
change" show a trend towards embracing new
ideas and being responsive to different
circumstances.
```

These patterns reveal that successful change management is less about stringent plans and more about people, leadership, and an adaptive approach that considers the unique aspects of each organization and change initiative.

These were the follow-up prompts:

the next question was "what was the most difficult challenge you faced with respect to managing change?" there were 74 responses" analyze the data in the same way you did for the last question

the next question was "what are you most excited to learn about next year?" there were 74 responses analyze the data the same way you did for the other questions

the next question was "what would you like to see in a 'state of change management' report?" 74 responses analyze it the same way as the last question

Can you write me a blog post[1] that summarizes all four questions and provide insights about what change managers can do to be more effective given the data from the responses?

can you make me a 16:9 aspect ratio image that would fit as a featured image for that blog post?

This is what prompted me to write this book. The answers were long and I thought instead of a one-off blog post, it would be a good idea to capture this as I'm pretty sure it'd be useful for other change agents!

This next one is going to rock your world. I asked AI how it could help change management and one of the responses was "predictive analytics". By the way, the answer to this prompt is in Chapter 5 just in case you glossed over it.

Here are the prompts I used:

> *can you tell me more about how you can help with this point: Predictive Analysis and Planning: AI can predict potential challenges and outcomes of change initiatives by analyzing data trends. This helps in devising more effective strategies and reduces risks associated with changes.*

> *how would you need the data to be structured to help me figure out how this organizational reorganization would affect the teams and productivity and culture? (Which AI knew was a followup to one of the points it responded with)*

Here's the full exchange. First, how can AI help with predictive analytics:

∾

Absolutely, AI's capabilities in predictive analysis and planning can be immensely beneficial in the context of change management. Here's how AI can assist in this area:

1. Data-Driven Predictions: AI algorithms can process vast amounts of historical data to identify patterns and trends that may not be apparent to humans. This includes analyzing past change initiatives, their success rates, challenges encountered, and the factors that influenced their outcomes.

2. Scenario Modelling: AI can simulate various scenarios based on different inputs and variables. This helps in understanding the potential impacts of different change strategies and choosing the one with the highest likelihood of success. For example, AI can model how changes in organizational structure or process modifications might affect productivity or employee satisfaction.

3. Risk Identification and Mitigation: AI tools can proactively identify potential risks in change initiatives. By analyzing factors such as employee sentiment, market trends, and operational data, AI can highlight areas of concern, allowing managers to address these risks before they become problematic.

4. Customized Strategy Development: Based on the predictive analysis, AI can recommend tailored strategies for change management. This can include identifying the most effective communication channels, the best timing for implementing changes, and the right pacing for different phases of the change process.

5. Enhanced Decision-Making: With AI's ability to analyze complex data sets, change managers can make more informed decisions. AI's insights can complement human judgment, leading to more nuanced and effective planning.

6. Monitoring and Adjustment: AI doesn't just predict and plan; it can also monitor the progress of change initiatives in real-

time. This allows for ongoing adjustments to the strategy, ensuring that the change management process remains aligned with organizational goals and external conditions.

7. Stakeholder Analysis: AI can analyze stakeholder data to predict how different groups within the organization might react to the change. Understanding stakeholder attitudes and concerns early in the process can inform more effective stakeholder engagement strategies.

8. Predictive Analytics for Training Needs: AI can predict which departments or employees might need additional training or support during the change process, allowing for proactive planning of training programs.

9. Forecasting Outcomes: AI can provide forecasts about the outcomes of change initiatives, including potential increases in efficiency, cost savings, and improvements in employee engagement, helping to build a business case for the change.

10. Continuous Learning: As AI systems are exposed to more data over time, their predictions and recommendations become more accurate and refined, leading to continuous improvement in change management strategies.

By leveraging these capabilities, AI can significantly enhance the planning and execution of change initiatives, making them more data-driven, strategic, and adaptable to changing conditions.

And the answer to my followup about scenario modelling:

To effectively utilize AI for analyzing how an organizational reorganization would affect teams, productivity, and culture, the data should be structured comprehensively and systematically. Here are key data types and structuring approaches you'd need:

Employee Data:

- Demographics: Age, gender, tenure, role, department, and location.
- Performance Metrics: Historical performance data, productivity metrics, and any KPIs (Key Performance Indicators) relevant to each role.
- Training and Skills: Records of skills, qualifications, and training completed.

Team and Departmental Data:

- Current and Historical Structure: Composition of teams, reporting lines, and departmental structures both before and after the reorganization.
- Workload and Capacity Data: Information on current projects, workload distribution, and resource allocation.
- Collaboration Networks: Data on inter-departmental collaborations and communication patterns.

Cultural and Engagement Data:

- Employee Engagement Surveys: Data from past surveys including job satisfaction, engagement levels, and cultural aspects.
- Turnover Rates: Historical turnover data, including reasons for leaving if available.
- Feedback and Sentiments: Qualitative data from exit interviews, internal forums, or any other feedback mechanisms.

Organizational Performance Data:

- Business Performance Metrics: Sales data, customer satisfaction scores, or other relevant business performance indicators.
- Operational Data: Efficiency metrics, process completion times, error rates, etc.

Change Implementation Data:

- Change Plans: Detailed plans of the proposed reorganization, including timelines and expected changes at each stage.
- Communication Records: Records of how the change was communicated, including employee town halls, newsletters, etc.

External Data (if relevant):

- Industry Benchmarks: Data on industry standards for productivity, employee satisfaction, etc.
- Economic Indicators: Any external economic factors that might influence organizational performance.

Data Structuring:

- Time-Stamped Records: Ensure all data is time-stamped to track changes over time.
- Standardized Formats: Data should be in a consistent format to facilitate analysis (e.g., CSV, Excel, SQL databases).
- Integration of Different Data Sources: Data from different sources should be integrated into a unified data model.

Ethical and Privacy Considerations:

- Anonymization: Personal identifiers should be removed to protect employee privacy.
- Compliance with Regulations: Ensure the data collection and processing complies with relevant data protection regulations (like GDPR).

Once structured effectively, AI algorithms can analyze this data to predict the impact of reorganization on team dynamics, productivity, and overall organizational culture. It can identify potential risks and opportunities, helping in creating a more informed and strategic approach to managing the change.

Finally, I wanted to know precisely what format the data would need to be in so I asked:

can you make me a template for adding the 'team and demographic' data for the organiational reorganization question I asked earlier?

Yes, spelling mistake and all! Here's what it created:

Sheet 1: Employee Demographics

Employee ID	Name	Age	Gender	Department	Role	Tenure (Years)	Location
001	John Doe	32	Male	Marketing	Manager	3	New York
002	Jane Smith	29	Female	Human Resources	Specialist	2	San Francisco
...	...	...	...	...	...	...	...

Sheet 2: Performance Metrics

Employee ID	Annual Review Score (1-5)	Project Completion Rate	Absenteeism Rate
001	4.2	95%	2%
002	3.8	88%	5%
...	...	...	...

Sheet 3: Training and Skills

Employee ID	Highest Qualification	Relevant Certifications	Skills
001	MBA	PMP, Google Analytics	Leadership, Analysis
002	B.A. Psychology	HR Management	Communication, HR
...	...	...	...

How cool is that?

Ideas for Prompts

It's hard to suggest prompts without knowing your specific context. Instead, here are ideas for prompts that you will need to modify a bit depending on what you need to analyze.

I am going to upload a spreadsheet of our last 10 email campaigns. The data includes the subject line, full content, open rates, click rates per link and the user. Can you tell me what's been the most popular, least popular etc etc.

I am the change manager on a large 3-year program supporting 12 teams, and 3 vendors. I am responsible for providing the program manager and executives with an update on how the 'change readiness' is going. I am going to upload the documents from all 12 teams and 3 vendors. Honestly, it's a bit messy but I'd like you to narrow down potential issues and ask me any questions you think an executive might have.

I did a 'change readiness' survey for <insert what the change is>. This change affects <these people> and the results I will upload are split by business vs IT and also by staff, managers, and leaders. Can you analyze it and give me insights into who's ready and who isn't? Also summarize points that show where people might be apprehensive, or what questions they have. After that, create an executive summary showing what percentage of people appear to have high confidence in this change working...etc etc.

Yes, your prompts can be that complicated and long. Remember, when analyzing data, you need to know what you want to get out of it but again, you can ask AI to help you ask it the right questions.

CHAPTER 15
COMMUNICATIONS

T here is some overlap with this section and the upcoming Content Creation chapter so I'll keep this section focused more on creating appropriate messages for the medium and for personalizing communications.

Let's start with understanding the effectiveness of your communications. I uploaded a CSV containing a list of all the newsletters I've sent out including the day they were sent, open rates, click rates, bounces and all the other data newsletter software typically has.

I asked:

> here is a csv of all the newsletter campaigns I've sent out, can you tell me which day of the week is the best for sending out campaigns?

GPT-4 told me the number of times I sent a campaign out on certain days but said it couldn't tell me which one was the most popular without more information. Since that information was already in the CSV, I said:

that spreadsheet contains open rates for each campaign. Can you use that data to tell me which days get the best open rates?

And it replied with:

Based on the open rates for each campaign, the average open rates for newsletters sent on different days of the week are as follows:

1. Monday: 37.37%
2. Wednesday: 35.92%
3. Thursday: 34.24%
4. Tuesday: 33.52%
5. Friday: 31.52%

From this data, Monday appears to be the best day for sending out campaigns in terms of achieving the highest average open rates, followed by Wednesday and Thursday. Keep in mind that these results are based on the data you've provided and can vary depending on various factors like audience, content, and overall email strategy

This is a simple example, but here are other prompts you can use:

that spreadsheet has the dates the campaigns were sent out, can you generate a chart showing the open rates over time as well as the subscriber trend over time?

can you find which links get clicked on the most across all campaigns? Include the campaign name and the date it was sent in your response.

find which newsletter led to the most unsubscribes

Most newsletter services will give you reports, so yes, you can do this manually. Once you want to evaluate your overall comms strategy, it's useful to be able to instantly get insights across all of your campaigns.

The coolest thing with using AI for communications is personalized messaging. Here's how to do it.

First, give GPT-4 some information about your audience:

I am going to give you three personas. These are the personas that represent the majority of people on my mailing list. I am writing a book on using AI in change management and would like you to create 3 versions of a newsletter. 1) targeted at change managers who are experienced, curious about ai but are not technical at all. 2) change managers who are experienced, curious about AI and work on technology projects. they know enough to carry on a conversation about technology, but they are not developers who understand the intricate details. 3) agile coaches who generally work in software, they may not be hardcore developers but they will understand technical jargon. before I give you the intention and ideas for the newsletter, do you have any questions about the audience?

In my case, it responded with:

Thank you for outlining the personas for your newsletter audience. To create tailored newslet-

ters for each group, I have a few clarifying
questions:

1. Tone and Complexity: For each persona, what
   level of complexity and technical detail
   would be most appropriate? For instance,
   should the newsletter for the first persona
   (non-technical change managers) avoid
   technical jargon entirely, while the one
   for the third persona (agile coaches) can
   be more technical?
2. Specific Interests or Pain Points: Are
   there any specific interests or common pain
   points for each persona that should be
   addressed or highlighted in the
   newsletters?
3. Call to Action: What is the primary goal or
   call to action for each newsletter? For
   example, is it to inform, to encourage the
   purchase of your book, to engage in a
   discussion, or something else?
4. Content Preferences: Do these personas have
   any known preferences for certain types of
   content, such as case studies, tips and
   tricks, industry updates, or personal
   anecdotes?
5. Newsletter Length and Format: Do you have a
   preferred length or format for these
   newsletters? For example, some audiences
   might prefer shorter, more concise content,
   while others might appreciate more detailed
   and in-depth information.

Understanding these aspects will help in crafting newsletters that resonate well with each of your target personas.

Understandable. Here's where you have options. You can prompt GPT-4 individually or create a spreadsheet with your information. For example, the spreadsheet could have one row per persona with the details for each. I decided to simply prompt GPT-4 with:

1) for agile agile coaches, the tone can be light, informal and fun. For both change manager personas, it should be more formal.

2) for both change manager personas, they'd be interested in 'demystifying ai' because they're not that technical for the most part. they are probably be thrown into AI projects without knowing much about it. For agile coaches, they just want to be on the bleeding edge because they're typically early adopters of new tech.

3) call to action for all is to download the book!

4) change managers love case studies and social proof, agile coaches just want the idea and want to try it out. agile coaches love stories

5) it should be a teaser. maybe 2 or 3 paragraphs with the goal that it'll entice them enough to click the links in the email

Here's what GPT-4 generated :

Based on your detailed description of the personas and their preferences, here are three tailored versions of a newsletter teaser for each group. The goal is to entice readers to download your book on using AI in change management.

Newsletter for Non-Technical Change Managers

Subject: Unveiling AI in Change Management — No Tech Expertise Required!

Content: Dear Change Leader,

Ever felt bewildered by AI jargon on your projects? You're not alone! Our new book, "AI in Change Management: A No-Nonsense Guide," demystifies AI for professionals like you. Discover how AI can be a game-changer in your change management initiatives, all explained in simple, jargon-free language. Delve into real-world case studies where AI has revolutionized change management, offering insights and proven strategies for success.

Don't let AI be a mystery any longer. Download your copy now and lead change with confidence!

[Download the Book]

Newsletter for Technically Proficient Change Managers

Subject: Elevate Your Tech Projects: AI and Change Management Uncovered

Content: Greetings,

As a change manager on the frontline of technology projects, understanding AI's role is crucial. "AI in Change Management: Integrating New Tech with Ease" is your resource for bridging the gap between AI and effective change implementation. This book provides a straightforward exploration of AI in a tech-savvy yet accessible manner, enabling you to hold confident conversations about AI in your projects.

Gain insights from case studies that demonstrate AI's impact in technology-driven change environments. Ready to elevate your projects with AI?

[Download the Book]

Newsletter for Agile Coaches

Subject: Stay Ahead: Explore AI's Cutting-Edge Role in Agile Environments

Content: Hey Agile Enthusiasts!

Dive into the world of AI with our latest read, "AI Meets Agile: Innovating at the Speed of Change." This book is a playground of ideas, showcasing how AI is shaping the future of agile methodologies. Packed with engaging stories and innovative concepts, it's tailored for those who thrive on the bleeding edge of technology.

Embrace AI in your agile journey and be the trendsetter in your field. Are you ready to explore?

[Download the Book]

~

A good starting point, but not perfect. They all sound a little too 'sales focused'. I'm going to stop here, but this is an idea of what you could try next:

could you make another version for each one and make it sound less like a sales pitch? both change manager personas will want to get a basic understanding of ai and will want to know how it can help them with change management. the agile coaches will want to understand how ai can help them help the teams they're coaching

GPT-4 generated another version for each persona and I again prompted it:

add this content to each one: This book will help you: understand what ai is, and is not, what impact technology has on organizational change, and how to use AI on change projects

And here was the response:

～

Certainly! Here are the updated versions of the newsletters with the added content highlighting the key benefits of the book.

Newsletter for Non-Technical Change Managers

Subject: Discover How AI Can Simplify Your Change Management Process

Content: Hello Change Leaders,

Navigating the world of AI can seem daunting, especially when your expertise lies outside the realm of technology. Our latest book, "AI in Change Management: Simplifying the Complex," is crafted to help you gain a fundamental understanding of AI and its practical applications in change management. We break down complex concepts into easily digestible insights, helping you see how AI can streamline and enhance your change initiatives.

This book will help you:

- Understand what AI is, and is not.
- Comprehend the impact technology has on organizational change.
- Learn how to use AI on change projects effectively.

Explore at your own pace and discover how AI can be a valuable ally in your change management journey.

[Learn More About the Book]

Newsletter for Technically Proficient Change Managers

Subject: Integrating AI in Change Management: A Tech-Savvy Exploration

Content: Dear Colleagues,

As change managers in tech-driven environments, understanding the nuances of AI can be a significant asset. "AI in Change Management: Bridging Technology and Strategy" offers a comprehensive look into how AI can be integrated into your change management practices. This book is designed to enhance your existing tech knowledge, providing insights into AI's role in facilitating efficient change processes.

This book will assist you in:

- Gaining a clear understanding of AI's capabilities and limitations.
- Exploring the influence of technology on organizational change.

- Applying AI effectively in your change management projects.

Join us on a journey of discovery where technology meets strategy, and empower your change management efforts with AI.

[Dive into the Book]

Newsletter for Agile Coaches

Subject: Enhancing Agile Coaching with AI Insights

Content: Hey Agile Community,

As agile coaches, staying ahead in the tech landscape is key to guiding your teams effectively. Our new publication, "AI for Agile: A Coach's Companion," delves into how artificial intelligence is reshaping agile coaching. Discover tools and strategies where AI supports agile practices, helping you provide better guidance and solutions to the teams you coach.

Through this book, you will:

- Develop a solid understanding of what AI really is.
- Learn about the impact of technology on organizational change.
- Discover ways to incorporate AI into your agile projects.

Embark on this enlightening journey to bring a fresh perspective to your coaching toolkit with the power of AI.

```
[Explore the Book's Insights]
```

Personalized Communications

The possibilities are endless here. For example, here's a prompt you can use if you're a fan of David Kearsey's Temperaments:

> can you write me 4 emails targeted at executives and use language and a tone that is suitable for each of these 4 temperaments:
>
> 1) guardian - be brief, be bold be gone,
>
> 2) idealist - tell me what this would mean for the people
>
> 3) artisan - informal, experimental tone
>
> 4) rational - very logical and structured.
>
> I am going to send them the executive summary but want to customize it in language that speaks to them

The key here is knowing your audience. GPT-4 knows about all temperament and personality type models so you can ask it to create communications specifically for each one.

Ideas for Prompts

Both of the examples above are reasonably simple, but here are some advanced ideas that go a bit deeper.

> I am going to upload 5 articles that were the most popular on our intranet this week. Can you create a summary of each and create a message for stakeholders, managers and staff? Executives want to

know <what do they want?>, managers want <what do managers want?> and staff would care about <what would they care about>

I am going to upload our communications plan, can you analyze it for me and give me feedback about the frequency of the messages. I previously gave you a report with the history of our campaigns, also suggest when we should send the next <10> messages and what content we might want to include

here are the replies to our last communications campaign, can you analyze it and tell me what the general sentiment is, what people's concerns are and suggest what we should send next time? Use the plan I uploaded earlier and the history of our campaigns I also uploaded to make sure we're not resending the same information too many times

I was on vacation for a week and there was a long email thread about a risk with the project. Can you highlight the most important parts I should look at that pertain to business readiness? Also suggest who in the thread I should talk to. (obviously there will be personal information in this thread but if you use GPT-4 only, your chat will be available to you only.

CHAPTER 16
PROJECT AND CHANGE MANAGEMENT ASSISTANT

I have SO many ideas and examples to share!

From my experience, these are most of the project and change management activities I've had to do:

- Update documentation.
- Provide status updates.
- Review risks, issues, blockers.
- Facilitate meetings, and provide notes.
- Doing surveys and gathering insights.

There's obviously more, but for this chapter, I'll focus on these because I've covered other things like training, content creation, and data analysis in other chapters. The important part about the items I picked is that the analysis AI can do is phenomenal.

I wish AI would have been around in the mid-2000s when I was using A3 reports as a foundation for my change activities. Now I use change canvases, but the concept is more or less the same.

In the mid-2000s, I was working for a medium-sized company with about 1200 employees as an agile coach. We were working across the organization, but mostly with their 16 teams in the technology group. Long story short, every quarter we would look back on the previous quarter, see what happened, update the docs, create status reports, and then start working on the new A3 for the next quarter.

The A3 was reasonably simple, the data that fed into it was not. There was too much and it was hard for leaders to digest. I still have those A3 reports almost 15 years later because I'm a pack-rat so I scrubbed out any sensitive data, names etc and used GPT-4 like this:

Do you know what the A3 report, as created by Toyota is?

It replied yes, and explained it to me.

If I give you an A3 document that has accomplishments of a 90-day plan, details about the data on the a3 and then recommendations, can you format it in a concise way? This would be targeted at c-level executives to help them understand the most important accomplishments, barriers to improvement and recommendations for next steps. It's just a big, messy google doc so tell me if you need it structured differently.

It gave me some details for uploading the data:

～

```
Yes, I can help format your A3 document into a
concise and clear summary for C-level executives.
To do so, I would typically focus on distilling
the information into key highlights and action-
able insights. Here's a general structure you
might consider:
```

Title: A clear title indicating the subject of the 90-day plan.

Background/Context: A brief statement about the context and objective of the plan.

Key Accomplishments:

- List the most significant achievements from the plan.
- Include quantifiable results or qualitative impacts where possible.

Barriers to Improvement:

- Identify any obstacles or challenges encountered during the period.
- Briefly analyze the cause or impact of these barriers.

Recommendations for Next Steps:

- Provide clear and actionable recommendations for moving forward.
- Include priorities, responsible parties, and any necessary resources or changes.

Summary/Conclusion: A succinct wrap-up emphasizing the overall progress and future focus.

When crafting this document, it's crucial to ensure that the language is precise and to the point, avoiding unnecessary details that might distract from the main message. Visual aids like charts or graphs can be very effective in conveying complex data or trends quickly. If you provide the content of the A3 document, I can help format it into this structured summary.

~

I then copy and pasted a 7-page google doc that I won't share here, and here is how GPT-4 summarized it:

~

Here is a concise and structured summary of the provided A3 document tailored for C-level executives:

A3 Summary for 90-Day Plan

Title: Agile and Quality Improvement 90-Day Review

Background/Context: Initiated in July 2009, the focus was on enhancing production capability by decreasing failure demand due to the high demand on MDS reducing capacity for progress on strategic initiatives. Significant strides have been made in team Agile processes.

Key Accomplishments:

- Code Health Metrics: Implemented Sonar, Findbugs, PMD; created 439 unit tests; moved to trunk development and standardized DEV image.
- Testing Automation: Proof of Concept (PoC) on automated testing framework; plan for template DB implementation.
- Coaching Initiatives: Product Owner Training across teams; technical study

groups on refactoring; cross-functional pairing; consistent retrospectives.
* Scrum Implementation: Introduced end of sprint demos, backlog grooming, feature development from users' perspective.

Barriers to Improvement:

* Quality & Technical: Inadequate automated testing leading to long regression phases; prevalent mini-waterfall practices; code changes during regression.
* Productivity: Diversion of resources from MDS impacted improvement capacity; constantly changing priorities.
* People/Learning Culture: Early return from maternity leave; insufficient learning culture.

Recommendations for Next Steps:

* Testing Automation: Implement acceptance testing framework and automate regression.
* Engineering Initiatives: Refactor frequently changed code areas; isolate code to enable componentized releases.
* Product Initiatives: Revise release schedule and create measurable product goals.
* Coaching Initiatives: Continue with workshops and study groups; host open space for product and engineering.
* Organizational Changes: Form dedicated teams for technical improvement and Agile transition; additional technical coaching;

dedicate a full day for open space learning.

Summary/Conclusion: The 90-day plan has led to a 20% accomplishment in improving code quality, testing automation, and scrum implementation. However, challenges remain in quality, productivity, and culture that need addressing through structured countermeasures and recommendations. Continued focus on Agile processes, automated testing, and organizational learning culture is critical for future success. Dedicated teams for improvement and ongoing coaching will be essential to carry the momentum forward.

~

Summaries are simple to create with any AI tool. I included plenty of examples in the data analysis chapter. Here's where it gets magical!

It took a few days and the time of 15 people (myself, the other coach and all the department managers) to create the next A3. Here's what I'd have done if AI existed back then:

> the goal of our transformation is to increase quality. There have been too many outages, and too many instances of long regression cycles due to poor testing practices. Most of the teams appreciate our help but the business executives are still annoyed that things take so long. Can you create an A3 report that suggests what we can do to increase quality given what we've done over the last 90 days?

This is what GPT-4 suggested

~

A3 Report: Quality Improvement Strategy

Title: Enhancing Quality through Agile and Testing Practices

Background/Context:

- Objective: Address the high incidence of outages and long regression cycles.
- Need: Improve quality to meet business expectations and reduce operational disruptions.
- Past Efforts: Past 90 days focused on code health, testing automation, and Agile process improvements.

Current Conditions:

- Outcomes of 90-Day Plan:
- Enhanced code health metrics implementation.
- Initiated a Proof of Concept for automated testing.
- Adopted Agile practices like scrum implementation and backlog grooming.
- Challenges:
- Persistent outages and extended regression cycles.
- Business dissatisfaction due to prolonged project timelines.

Root Cause Analysis:

- Quality Issues: Inadequate coverage and effectiveness of current testing practices.

- Technical Limitations: Lack of comprehensive automated testing.
- Process Gaps: Mini-waterfall practices hindering Agile adoption.

Countermeasures:

Enhance Automated Testing:

- Fully implement and integrate the automated testing framework.
- Increase the coverage and frequency of automated tests.

Refine Agile Processes:

- Strengthen Agile practices to reduce development cycle time.
- Enhance cross-functional collaboration for faster issue resolution.

Optimize Regression Testing:

- Develop a strategy to shorten regression cycles.
- Prioritize tests based on risk and impact.

Continuous Learning and Improvement:

- Conduct regular training and workshops on Agile and quality practices.
- Establish a feedback loop from business executives to understand their concerns and align strategies.

Plan for Implementation:

- Short-Term Goals (Next 30 days):
- Finalize and implement the automated testing framework.
- Conduct workshops on Agile methodologies and efficient testing practices.
- Medium-Term Goals (30-60 days):
- Evaluate and optimize regression testing processes.
- Initiate regular feedback sessions with business executives.
- Long-Term Goals (60-90 days):
- Review and assess the impact of implemented strategies.
- Adapt and refine approaches based on feedback and results.

Expected Outcomes:

- Reduction in the frequency and duration of outages.
- Shorter regression cycles and quicker time to market.
- Improved satisfaction from business executives and stakeholders.

Conclusion: This plan aims to build on the progress made in the last 90 days, focusing specifically on enhancing quality through better testing practices and more robust Agile processes. By addressing the root causes of quality issues and aligning closely with business expectations, the goal is to significantly reduce outages and improve overall operational efficiency.

∽

I would have projected this in the meeting room and asked the people if this was a sufficient strategy. The devil is always in the details, so there would be work to do but as far as taking what we already did and suggesting what to do next, GPT-4 was pretty close to what we actually did at that company.

Next, I would have taken the data we had from our original A3 which included support cases over time, defects reported by customers, efficacy of testing efforts (no, not number of test cases, that is useless!), and put that stuff into a spreadsheet.

After each week, or month I'd update the spreadsheet and include what we've done and what the outcomes were. Then I'd ask GPT-4:

Analyze this spreadsheet and generate an executive summary showing trends in defects reported by customers, support cases (and whatever other data I defined). Include the major activities the teams have done and generate insights about what has improved, and what still needs work.

Here is a profile of the CTO and CEO. These are the things they are concerned about <list the things>. Can you tell me what questions they might have about this plan? For each question you generate, can you write an answer based on something from the A3 report?

I am going to upload our last 1000 customer support requests. Analyze them and list the most common problems. We want to focus our testing efforts on what matters most to customers. After that, update the A3 you created with specifics about the areas we'll focus on.

I'll stop there as I could go on forever!

I remember those A3 sessions quite well. Hundreds and hundreds of hours, frustrations, document creation and more. Had we had this AI co-pilot, no pun intended, we'd have been able to plough through this in one afternoon.

Don't forget, it's the knowledge of the people in room that matters. They know the environment, systems, and have ongoing tacit knowledge about what we've done and what they think we should do. GPT-4 is just helping us organize things, which, now that I think of it, might have made me obsolete next quarter!

> *Spoiler alert, we eventually got fired anyway, but as consultants you expect that to happen. To be fair, it wasn't because of something we did, it was because a new SVP was hired and they wanted to exert their dominance and bring their own people in.*

Summarizing and Analyzing Meeting Notes

I uploaded an old picture from a retrospective I had with a few teams over 10 years ago:

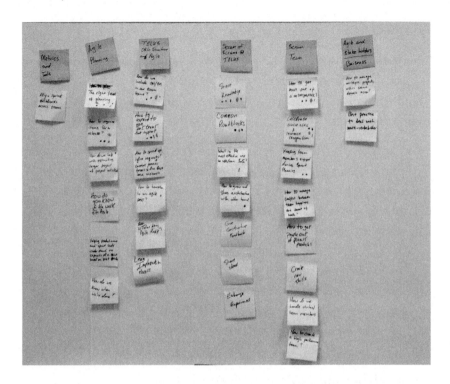

Personally, I don't usually document all of this stuff, but many change managers (or project managers) I know need to provide meetings notes, status updates and more. Usually the team manager wants them. Doing that stuff is a giant pain in the ass so here's how I prompted GPT-4 to help:

> *I held a retrospective for an agile transformation project I'm working on. I am going to upload the image of the output. The blue sticky notes are the category. The yellow sticky notes are the questions. The 'dots' on the cards represent the votes that question received. Can you format that data into a table with these columns: category, question, votes, suggestions. In the 'suggestions' column, if you can read the question, provide one or two short bullet points that would answer it. here's the image <uploaded the image>:*

I purposely picked an old image that is hard to read, and GPT-4 gave me a very long answer with how it was struggling to read the text so it retried a few times and explained what it could and couldn't do. Impressive.

So I uploaded a high-res version and said:

here's a higher resolution image, can you try again?

This is what is generated:

Category	Question	Votes	Suggestions
Metrics and Tools	Metrics Sprint dashboard across teams	1	- Consolidate dashboards for unified team metrics.
	How do you track your work in JIRA?	2	- Utilize JIRA boards and filters for task tracking.
Agile Planning	The right level of planning?	1	- Balance detail with flexibility; adjust as needed.
	How to organize items for release?	2	- Prioritize items based on strategic importance.
	How do you keep other projects aware of project status?	1	- Regular inter-project communication updates.
TELs & Org Structure & Agile	How to improve after-action reports for TELs?	1	- Focus on actionable insights and clear follow-ups.
Scrum of Scrums or TELs	What is the most effective way to run SoS?	3	- Focus on clear objectives and outcomes for SoS.
	Share knowledge!	1	- Create a knowledge-sharing platform or regular meetups.
Common Roadblocks	How to avoid over-architecting the solution?	2	- Implement iterative design with regular reviews.
	Give constructive feedback ↓	1	- Train in feedback techniques; foster open

Then I asked it to generate a summary for the manager. I'm not going to post that output because you've probably seen enough examples to know what it would look like.

The lesson here is, you can collaborate in Miro, Mural, in-person via sticky notes, or any combination and AI will help create whatever documents you need instantly.

Now combine this with some of the prompts from the other chapters and you're well on your way to getting your sanity back. The only evidence I can give for that is the fact that I have done all of the examples for this book in about 3 hours and I'm not even remotely tired yet.

Ideas for Prompts

I am going to upload the last 10, bi-weekly status reports. Create a summary about the progress that has been made that I can use in the quarterly status update. highlight major accomplishments and what risks exist

I created a strategic change canvas from Lean Change, do you know what this is? (GPT-4 should say, "of course I do, it's the greatest approach to change management ever!). I used flips charts and sticky notes and I want you to create a digital version. Using a table, or bulleted list is fine. The blue sticky notes represent the strategy box, the green sticky notes represent the 'whos affected' bot <etc>

I am working on <context of the project> one of the vendors sent a 5 page implementation update for the component our technical teams are using. I need to create a 'whats changed' report for them. I am lazy, can you do it for me?

I'm stuck. Leaders are pushing for the change to happen faster but people are busy and don't have time to participate in any of our change activities. Can you suggest a few things? Also, can you look at any feedback from surveys I've given you so far and let me know what previously worked?

I am going to upload a survey that I call a 'perspective map'. The questions are in the data and there is a column for 'role'. I have feedback from stakeholders, managers and team members. There are 700 rows of data. I would like you to analyze areas where people are aligned and areas where there is a difference in perception between the stakeholders, managers and staff

Again, I could go on forever. I highly suggest that you try these out. I have included enough prompts that should show you possibilities. More importantly, I hope these prompts show you how to structure your prompts:

- Add context.
- Describe the data.
- Ask for what you are looking for.
- Ask if the bot needs more information.

Remember, go to https://leanchange.org/ai as I will be continually updating content, and ideally, experiments people have tried!

CHAPTER 17
BETTER MEETINGS

I am taking the lazy way out for this chapter. I asked GPT-4:

how can you help make our meetings more efficient and effective?

It replied with:

~

To make meetings more efficient and effective, AI like me can assist in several ways:

1. Agenda Preparation and Optimization: Before the meeting, I can help you draft a comprehensive and focused agenda. You can provide me with key topics or goals, and I can suggest a structured agenda that ensures all critical points are addressed efficiently.

2. Participant Preparation: I can generate briefs or summaries on meeting topics to circulate among participants beforehand. This ensures everyone comes prepared, reducing the time needed for context-setting during the meeting.

3. Real-Time Note-Taking and Summarization: During the meeting, AI tools can transcribe discussions in real-time. I can then summarize the key points, decisions, and action items, ensuring that important details are captured and readily available for reference.

4. Meeting Analysis for Continuous Improvement: Post-meeting, I can analyze the content of the discussion to identify areas that could be streamlined or improved in future meetings. For example, highlighting topics that consumed disproportionate time or areas where clarity was lacking.

5. Action Item Tracking and Follow-Up: I can help identify and list action items from the meeting, assign them to respective team members, and even draft follow-up reminders or emails to ensure accountability and progress.

6. Scheduling and Coordination: I can assist in finding suitable times for meetings by analyzing participants' availability, helping to schedule meetings at times that work for all involved parties.

7. Facilitating Remote Collaboration: In case of virtual meetings, I can provide tips and

best practices for effective remote collaboration, ensuring that the meeting is productive even when participants are not physically present together.

8. FAQs and Instant Information Retrieval: If there are recurring questions or need for instant information during meetings, I can quickly provide answers or data, reducing delays in decision-making.

9. Customized Recommendations: Based on the nature of your meetings and specific challenges, I can offer tailored advice. For instance, if your meetings often run overtime, I can suggest time management techniques or ways to keep discussions on track.

10. Feedback Collection and Analysis: After the meeting, I can help design and analyze feedback surveys to understand participants' perspectives and identify areas for improvement.

Remember, the effectiveness of AI in enhancing meeting efficiency largely depends on how you integrate these tools into your meeting processes and the willingness of participants to engage with them.

I wanted GPT-4 to generate that list because you'll need to look at other AI tools, or GPT-4 plugins, that will allow you to:

• Create searchable transcripts.

- Create subtitles or do translations.
- Provide real-time insights during meetings.

These are the tools I've used and I'll provide a few options because for some of you, putting your content on the internet might not be a good idea!

Vimeo

Vimeo generates captions and subtitles automatically. You can download the files in VTT format. That's just a fancy term for a different type of text file. You can embed Vimeo videos so it's easy to create searchable transcripts for single videos.

You could take that transcript and add it to a spreadsheet, or Airtable, categorize and tag each row with the meeting purpose, transcript, tags, date etc and then feed GPT-4 that info. Now you have an 'ask our team meetings' bot.

Noty.ai

I mentioned this previously, Noty.AI works as a plugin in Google Meet, Zoom, Zapier, Slack and more. I used it in Zoom and once connected, it automatically does everything for you, and gives you a way to ask it to summarize data from the transcript.

Again, same problem, this will work great from video to video, but you'd still have to do something if you wanted a completely searchable, and historical reference.

Other notable Noty.ai features include:

- Automatic summary emails when using Gmail
- To-do lists and summaries
- Private and collaborative folders
- Customized language models

Rev.com

This will again create transcripts and also translations with descriptive text. That means if accessibility matters to you, Rev.com works perfectly.

Ideas for Prompts

To use these prompts, you need to do a bit of work first. You can use the tools above to prepare your data, and then you would need to collect feedback from your meetings. A spreadsheet, or Airtable table with this info should work:

- Meeting subject
- Meeting date
- Short overview
- Transcript
- Attendees
- Questions asked
- Action items
- Meeting feedback

Then ask:

what was the sentiment about the usefulness of our last 5 meetings?

what did people like? Not like?

analyze the last 5 meetings where we did some activities and tell me which activities people liked the most.

what are the most frequent complaints people have about our meetings? for each one, can you suggest what we could try?

what are the most common questions people ask in our status update meetings?

I missed the status update meeting on January 5, can you tell me what happened?

Once you have the data you want, and in a structured format, you can also repurpose the prompts from the data analysis chapter.

CHAPTER 18
CONTENT CREATION

I saved this to last on purpose. By now you should have a solid understanding of how to craft prompts so I am going to focus more on prompt construction and other AI tools that will help you create content, not just GPT-4.

I'm not going to paste in responses here, instead, I encourage you to head over the chat.openai.com and try them out!

This is how you structure your prompts to get the most out of interacting with AI:

Clear Objective: Start by clearly stating your objective. What do you want to achieve with this interaction? For example, "I need assistance in creating a project plan," or "I'm looking for information about the latest trends in renewable energy."

Specific Details: Provide specific details relevant to your query. This includes any context or background information that might help in generating a more accurate response. For instance, if you're asking for a project plan, mention the type of project, its scope, key milestones, and any constraints.

Direct Questions: If you have specific questions, phrase them directly. Instead of saying, "I'm thinking about market trends," ask, "What are the current market trends in the electric vehicle industry?"

Desired Format: Specify the format you prefer for the response. Do you want a detailed report, a summary, a list, step-by-step instructions, or something else? For example, "Please provide a summary of the key factors affecting market trends."

Tone and Style: If the tone or style is important (for example, if the response is for public consumption), mention this. Say something like, "I'd like the response to be formal and suitable for a business audience."

Any Limitations or Boundaries: If there are certain aspects or angles you want to avoid, or specific boundaries to adhere to, mention them. For example, "Please exclude any financial advice or recommendations in your response."

Follow-Up Clarity: If you're building on previous questions or continuing a conversation, briefly summarize the key points from earlier interactions to maintain context. For instance, "In our last discussion about renewable energy, you mentioned solar power trends. Can you elaborate on the current innovations in solar energy technology?"

Closing Request for Additional Information: End with an open-ended request for additional information if needed, like "Is there anything else I should know about this topic?" or "Can you suggest additional resources for further reading?"

Here's an example:

Objective: I need to develop a marketing strategy for our new eco-friendly product line.

Details: Our products include biodegradable utensils and recycled paper bags. The target market is environmentally conscious consumers in the urban areas of California.

Question: What are effective marketing strategies for reaching this audience?

Format: I would like a list of strategies, each with a brief explanation.

Tone: The response should be professional and data-driven.

Limitations: Avoid discussing price-based promotions, as our focus is on quality and sustainability.

Previous Interaction: In our last conversation, you mentioned social media as a key marketing tool. Can you include how social media can be leveraged for eco-friendly products?

Additional Information: Are there any recent success stories of similar products in the market?

You can simplify this more. A good prompt contains:

- A little context.
- A bit about your audience (or you).
- Specific details about what you want.

I would start there. Once you have those 3 things, it's easy enough to follow-up with more prompts to refine it.

Follow-up Prompts

You don't always need to be that specific, depending on what you want AI to create for you. Once it generates some content, you can ask it:

can you shorten that?

can you make a summary in bullet points?

can you write 4 versions of that, 1) more humorous 2) more formal 3) less technical sounding 4) targeted at <this role>

can you create <number> subject lines for an email that would get people to open it?

can you create me a featured image for that?

oh, can you make a square version of that same image?

Forget what I previously told you, I am going to upload an image, can you interpret the meaning for me?

I'm going to upload a sketch. I would like you to create me a minimalist icon that represents a conversation between two people. I would like it to be simple and in black and white.

I didn't like <this aspect> of that image, can you try again?

Can you create a similar looking icon, but instead make it represent someone thinking?

Creating Images

There are plenty of AI tools that can help you create images. The most popular are Mid Journey and Dall-E.

At the time of writing this, image creation works spectacularly for creative work and fails miserably for most business related tasks that would be useful for us. Here's an example, I asked the GPT-4 plugin InfoGraph Creator how many videos were added to the internet every day. It replied with this:

As of 2024, about 3.7 million videos are uploaded to YouTube every day. This includes a vast array of content, from short-form videos like YouTube Shorts, which receive 30 billion daily views, to longer content. In total, 500 hours of video content are uploaded to YouTube every minute, contributing to the platform's extensive and diverse range of videos

As another example, I asked it to generate the book summary that is on the back cover of this book. After it did that, I asked it to create a book cover:

I loved it! But I wanted a flat image with no text. I spent about a half an hour trying to re-create that same image with no text using a ton of prompts:

> can you re-create that exact same image I uploaded without any text and in 2d as a flat image. I like the lightbulb imagery and the open hands underneath as well as the icons that are around the light-bulb

> can you re-create that exact same image, but make it a flat image so I can import it into my book formatting software?

can you make me an image: it's about using ai in change manage-
ment. I would like it to be modern, colourful and when people see
it, it'll inspire them with possibilities about what AI can do for them

try again using an 'idea generator' metaphor. you can include a
light-bulb with icons that represent ideas around it

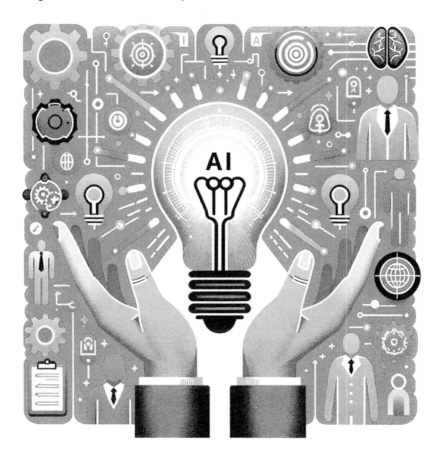

So I tried something different. I uploaded the original image it
created and asked:

I am going to upload an image, can you describe it to me?

The image depicts a large, luminous lightbulb that is held aloft by two open human hands. The lightbulb is a metaphorical tree of ideas and innovation, with its upper half transformed into a vibrant, autumn-colored tree with leaves. On the left side of the tree, intricate gear mechanisms can be seen, symbolizing technology and mechanization, blending into the branches. Surrounding the lightbulb tree are various icons and elements that float against a blue background, including a clock, compass, documents, a globe, a bookshelf with books, and more, all suggesting themes of knowledge, navigation, time management, and global connectivity. These elements together convey a concept of growth, innovation, and the synthesis of nature, technology, and human creativity in a dynamic balance.

can you make me an alternate version of that? use the same look and feel and make it portrait?

Much better, but still not what I wanted so I paid somebody on Fivvr to re-create it.

There's a hidden tip in GPT-4's ability to create images. When you download the image, the file name is actually the full prompt that it used to make Dall-E generate the image.

For the first image, the prompt was:

> DALL·E 2024-01-11 22.39.34 - An infographic illustrating the daily video uploads on YouTube in 2024. The main headline should be 'YouTube Upload Statistics 2024'. Key points to in

For the second image, the prompt was:

> DALL·E 2024-01-11 22.40.57 - A simplified infographic on YouTube video uploads in 2024, with a minimalist design. Headline_ 'YouTube 2024_ A Day in Numbers'. Include these three k

The filenames are cutoff, but that at least can give you a clue for prompts you could create.

Medium Specific Content

GPT-4 knows all current social media channels so you can create content for each easily. Let's say you're working on a major revision for a software project. You've already received a feature sheet and product documentation and you've been tasked with creating a summary about what's changed.

Let's assume you've use the detailed prompt template in this chapter and GPT-4 created a page-long piece of content. Here's how you can prompt it again to create more content:

> *Create me:*
>
> *5 blurbs for each social network: facebook, linkedin, X.*
>
> *Generate a video script that would fit into a 45 second TikTok, YouTube, and Instagram short. Format each script so it's relevant to those platforms.*
>
> *Generate a two-minute script that would be suitable for an explainer video.*

Here are the last 20 customer support comments, can you create an FAQ and use the new product data sheet I uploaded to answer them? If there are no sufficient answers to be found, let me know and I'll create them myself.

I imagine you might think some of this stuff isn't the responsibility of the change manager. Well, it depends on context. Many moons ago I found myself sub-contracted by a consulting firm that sold a 40-day engagement for a change consultant to help with an organizational transformation.

After a fantastic liftoff, a week later the entire dynamic changed. I have no idea what happened, but the leaders made a complete 180 and were not interested at all. So I basically had 35 days to kill. I felt like a hired handy-person from an online ad as I wandered around from team to team looking for things I could help out with.

My role was a change role and I ended up doing so many different things like researching how to merge code repositories, helping marketing re-organize how they worked together, doing adhoc training sessions and more. It was brutal. Fun, but brutal.

I have always believed the role of a change agent is to work in the whitespace and help with whatever needs to get done to make progress towards a goal. The more well-rounded we are, the more likely we're able to adapt to any context. The more we can get ahead of AI, which sounds nuts considering how fast it evolves, the more we'll be able to help our organizations make the most of it.

CHAPTER 19
WHAT'S NEXT?

T he AI landscape will have definitely changed by the time you've read this, but conceptually, it's simple:

- Talk to AI like it's a human, not a robot.
- Remember that AI 'stays in context', meaning you don't have to give it the same instructions over and over again.
- If you don't know how to prompt it, ask it.
- It'll always be as good as the data it's trained on, how its algorithms work and how you instruct and prompt it.
- Every piece of software on the planet is going to add AI capabilities.

This book is just the beginning. It will live on at https://leanchange.org/ai and it'll stay specific to change management. At that URL you'll find:

- The 'Ask Lean Change' bot.
- The State of Change Management bot.

- Over time, more tools and input from change managers so we can build a repository of good ideas for using AI, stories, change challenges and more.

I've been collecting change challenges, lean coffee questions, stories and more since the first version of Lean Change Management in 2012. AI is going to help me analyze all of this data and keep innovating in what change managers actually want, what challenges they're having and what's actually helping.

Lastly, because there are too many AI tools and plugins to list, I'll keep a free repository of them, but only keep ones that are relevant to change management.

Thanks for taking the time to read, or skim, this book, you're always welcome to share your feedback at leanchange.org/ai

CHAPTER 20
STATE OF CHANGE
MANAGEMENT

You can join our ongoing AI in Change Management survey at https://leanchange.org/ai.

It's been incorporated into our State of Change Management Custom GPT at https://chat.openai.com/g/g-LıBkZlaEs-state-of-change-management

State of AI in Change Management Survey

1. What advice would you give other change agents about AI?
2. What community do you belong to?
3. What about AI is the most confusing for you?
4. How have you used AI in change management?
5. How many years of experience in change do you have?
6. How do you think AI will change change management?
7. What are you skeptical about with respect to using AI in change management?
8. How technical are you?
9. What questions would you like this survey to answer for you?

Here are some things you can ask it:

What do change agents think about using AI in change management?

What's the general sentiment towards using ai in change management?

Tell me about the demographics of the respondents.

Where can I take the surveys?

It learns at more people interact with it so get creative with your questions!

State of Change Management Survey

Questions asked:

1. What's the most important lesson you learned about change management this past year?
2. What was the most difficult challenge you faced with respect to managing change this past year?
3. In a change management context, what are you most excited about learning in the future?
4. Any other comments?
5. What's your level of experience in change management? This is too complex of an answer to distill into 5 buckets, but do your best!
6. Why did you select that level?
7. Which community do you most closely associate yourself with?
8. Other community
9. What information would you want to see in a State of Change 'report'? (Comment box)
10. Completed Survey Date

You can ask the GPT any questions you want, and it can mix the results from both surveys if you want. If you want specific insights into either, make sure you ask it to reference either the AI survey, or the State of Change survey.

There is only about 100 responses at the time of finishing this book (January 18), but I think this approach is much better than annual *State of* reports because it's ongoing, there are no tool or method questions and since it's real-time, it'll always be up to date.

Both surveys include the date the entry was received so you can ask it specific date questions as well.

We only collected responses for the State of Change survey in 2019 so most of the data is from there, or after 2024.

Thanks for taking the time to read this book! I'll leave you with GPT-4's sentiment analysis of what change agents think about using AI in Change Management:

∾

The general sentiment in the responses from the "AI in Change Management" survey can be characterized as cautiously optimistic and curious. Here's a breakdown of the overall mood:

Optimism and Enthusiasm: Respondents show a clear interest in the potential of AI to enhance change management practices. They mention using AI for tasks like sentiment analysis, training course development, and data analysis, indicating a belief in AI's utility.

Caution and Skepticism: Alongside optimism, there's a notable caution about the limitations and challenges of AI. Concerns are raised about AI's unpredictability, the need for proper understanding and implementation, and skepticism about the maturity of organizations in using AI responsibly.

Advice and Open-mindedness: Respondents advise other change agents to experiment with AI and learn how to use it effectively. This indicates a trend towards embracing new technologies while also acknowledging the learning curve involved.

Concern about Misconceptions: There is a worry about misconceptions surrounding AI, particularly the fear that AI might replace human roles in change management. Respondents emphasize the importance of understanding what AI can and cannot do.

Recognition of AI's Limitations: Respondents express concerns about AI's ability to understand context and the need for skill-building among change agents to use AI effectively.

In summary, the general sentiment is one of cautious optimism with an emphasis on the need for understanding, responsible implementation, and skill development in the realm of AI and change management. The responses reflect a balance between recognizing the potential bene-fits of AI and acknowledging its current limita-tions and challenges.

I wonder how that will change as more change agents embrace and start using AI!

NOTES

1. About this Book

1. Levitin, Daniel J. The Organized Mind: Thinking Straight in the Age of Information Overload. Dutton, 2014. ISBN 978-0147516312.
2. https://leanchange.org/ai
3. https://sperocareerscanada.ca

3. Technology Takes Jobs...But

1. https://hbr.org/2021/11/automation-doesnt-just-create-or-destroy-jobs-it-transforms-them

4. AI 101

1. Arnold's famous character from the Terminator movies. He's still around near the end, but grossly outmatched!

6. Change Management Before AI

1. Little, Jason. Lean Change Management: Innovative Practices for Managing Organizational Change. Happy Melly Express, 2014. ISBN 978-0990466505.
2. https://leanchange.org/ai

7. Change Management After AI

1. https://leanchange.org/philosophy
2. 3 tools for using AI on YouTube https://youtu.be/74vIbxgRUZM

8. Why AI? Why Now?

1. https://leanchange.org/canvases
2. https://spacebarpress.com/
3. https://www.france24.com/en/tv-shows/science/20240117-world-s-first-news-network-powered-by-generative-ai-to-launch-in-march
4. https://changeagility.org

9. The Ethical Considerations of AI

1. https://www.law.com/corpcounsel/2024/01/17/ai-adoption-likely-to-spark-surge-in-corporate-litigation-of-all-stripes-in-2024/?slreturn=20240017152916
2. https://www.salon.com/2024/01/09/impossible-openai-admits-chatgpt-cant-exist-without-pinching-copyrighted-work/

10. Using Custom GPTs

1. Find this and more at https://leanchange.org/ai
2. https://botpress.com

11. Using No Code and APIs

1. https://airtable.com
2. https://zapier.com
3. https://make.com
4. https://bubble.io
5. Build Stuff with No Code https://www.youtube.com/channel/UCYfAjBxMx3e-qdqhtUuaJjTA

14. Data Analysis

1. https://blog.leanchange.org